PRENTICE-HALL
CONTEMPORARY PERSPECTIVES IN MUSIC EDUCATION SERIES
Charles Leonhard, Editor

Bennett Reimer
A PHILOSOPHY OF MUSIC EDUCATION

Robert Sidnell
BUILDING INSTRUCTIONAL PROGRAMS IN MUSIC EDUCATION

Charles Leonhard
THE ROLE OF METHOD IN MUSIC EDUCATION

Edwin Gordon
THE PSYCHOLOGY OF MUSIC TEACHING

Robert H. Klottman
ADMINISTRATION
The Dynamics of Change in Music Education

Richard Colwell
THE EVALUATION OF MUSIC TEACHING AND LEARNING

Clifford K. Madsen and Charles H. Madsen, Jr.
EXPERIMENTAL RESEARCH IN MUSIC

Daniel L. Wilmot
IMPROVING INSTRUCTION IN MUSIC EDUCATION

PRENTICE-HALL INTERNATIONAL, INC., London
PRENTICE-HALL OF AUSTRALIA, PTY. LTD., Sydney
PRENTICE-HALL OF CANADA, LTD., Toronto
PRENTICE-HALL OF INDIA PRIVATE LTD., New Delhi
PRENTICE-HALL OF JAPAN, INC., Tokyo

A PHILOSOPHY OF MUSIC EDUCATION

a philosophy
of music education

BENNETT REIMER

Music Department, Case Western Reserve University

PRENTICE-HALL, INC., Englewood Cliffs, New Jersey

© 1970 by PRENTICE-HALL, INC., Englewood Cliffs, New Jersey

Printed in the United States of America

C–13–663880–5
P–13–663872–4

Library of Congress Catalog Card No.: 74–95753

Current Printing (last digit):

10   9   8   7   6   5   4   3   2   1

To the memory of my father

foreword

Contemporary Perspectives in Music Education is a new series of professional books for music education. It establishes a pattern for music teacher education based on the areas of knowledge and processes involved in music education rather than on the levels and specializations in music education.

The areas of knowledge include philosophy of music education, psychology of music teaching, and research methods. The processes include program development, instruction, administration, supervision, and evaluation.

The basic premise of the series is that mastery of all of these processes and areas of knowledge is essential for the successful music educator regardless of his area of specialization and the level at which he teaches. The series presents in a systematic fashion information and concepts basic to a unified music education profession.

All of the books in the series have been designed and written for use in the undergraduate program of music teacher education. The pattern of the series is both systematic and flexible. It permits music education instructors at the college level to select one or more of the books as texts on the basis of their relevance to a particular course.

Bennett Reimer's *A Philosophy of Music Education* is the result of his continuing strong professional commitment to discovering the answers to some of the basic questions that face the music education profession in the twentieth century. His basic premise holds that a systematic statement of a philosophy of music education must be the result of a systematic investigation of the nature and value of music itself. This premise inevitably led him to the study of the aesthetics of music and subsequently to the adoption of the theoretical position in Aesthetics known as Absolute Expressionism.

Professor Reimer has done a masterful job of developing his theoretical position. In addition, he has accomplished a task immeasurably more difficult: he has succeeded in applying theory logically and consistently in answering the "practical" questions and in seeking solutions to problems that confront every music educator. In essence, he has treated the very problems and issues that cause a music educator to seek a sound philosophical basis for his professional life.

A Philosophy of Music Education is a distinguished work which is relevant to all levels and specializations in music education. I am confident that it will be uniquely effective in unifying the music education profession in our time and in providing a solid base for music education in the future.

Charles Leonhard

preface

Music instruction of one sort or another has been offered in American public schools for almost a century and a half. Throughout its long and eventful history music education has struggled with the problem of justifying its existence to the society on which it depends. Most of the arguments for the value of teaching and learning music have been directed toward the practical, utilitarian benefits to be derived, with an occasional nod toward the idea that art does something for the finer part of man's nature. Given the relative ease of discussing practical values, the difficulty of articulating aesthetic values, the immediate concern of American society with the practical and the diffuseness of its concern with the aesthetic, it is not surprising that justifications for music education have dealt richly with matters of outward utility and poorly with matters of inner significance.

In our own times a wide gulf has come to be recognized between success in quantitative aspects of life and failure in qualitative aspects. The human need for depth of experience, for a sense of meaningfulness and self-knowledge below the surface of everyday life, remains as pressing as it always has been, with clearer realization that this need will not be filled by technological advances. The contribution of the arts to the quality of human self-understanding can be at least as important now, if not much more so, than at any time in history.

Those concerned with music in education find themselves, therefore, in a position of potentially making a far more important, far more significant, far more practical contribution to society than was ever possible when aims for music education were primarily utilitarian and only secondarily aesthetic. In order for these aims to be reversed in importance an understanding must exist of the precise nature of aesthetic value, so that music educators can focus their efforts on sharing the aesthetic value of music with all children. It is very difficult at present to come to an understanding of how music education can become "aesthetic education," because so little has been written directly on this subject. The philosophy offered in this book is an attempt to supply the background of understanding out of which effective action can be generated.

B. R.

contents

A PHILOSOPHY OF MUSIC EDUCATION

CHAPTER
ONE

why have
a philosophy of
music education?

This book is based on a single, fundamental premise, which must be stated at the outset, because everything that follows is an attempt to explain its meaning and its applicability. The premise is that the nature and value of music education are determined by the nature and value of the art of music. Given human beings who are teaching and learning, and who are therefore constrained by all the factors bearing on teaching and learning, music education's character is a function of the character of music itself.

A philosophy of music education should be a systematic statement of music education's nature and value. According to the basic premise of this book, such a statement must come from an investigation of music's nature and music's value. If it is possible to present a convincing explanation of the fundamental nature of the art of music and the value of music in the lives of people, it becomes possible at the same time to present a convincing picture of music education's fundamental nature and its value in human life.

The field of thought which is concerned with questions of the nature and value of the arts is aesthetics. This book, therefore, will deal primarily with aesthetics (musical aesthetics in particular) but in a man-

1

ner which applies conceptions from aesthetics directly to the context of aesthetic education generally and music education in particular. It will be argued that this approach, while not the only possible one, is most suitable at this time in history. If music education in the present era could be characterized by a single, overriding purpose, one would have to say that this field is trying to become "aesthetic education." What is needed in order to fulfill this purpose is a philosophy which shows how and why music education is aesthetic in its nature and its value. This book is an attempt to provide such a philosophy.

It would be presumptuous in the extreme to imply that any philosophy, the present one included, can be taken to be a statement "for all time" or "for all people." On the one hand, music education, as everything else, changes with time, so that a philosophy which is convincing at one time is likely to be regarded as primarily of historical interest at another. The record of change in philosophies must be gleaned from representative writings over the years: unfortunately there have been few if any books devoted entirely to statements of music education philosophy. As one gets a sense of the changes in the nature of music education in history, it becomes impossible to entertain the notion that any single philosophy can be more than transient. This state of affairs keeps the would-be philosopher humble (a most salutary condition), but it does not relieve him of the obligation to articulate the underlying beliefs of the time in which he lives.

Above and beyond the effect of time and the changes time brings is the matter of the variability of beliefs at any one time in history. It is a truism that people differ in opinions about music education, and that these differences always have and always will exist. As this profession becomes more complex it is reasonable to assume that differences of philosophy will also become more complex. The philosopher must accept and even approve of this condition. But, again, the fact that no "one true answer" is possible or desirable does not remove the need for reasoned, careful, systematic statements which help make the field more understandable to all who are involved with it. A philosophy, then, must be conceived as being "of a time," and must also give recognition to the fact that it can only provide a point of departure for practitioners of that time.

And yet, having acknowledged the inherent limitations of any philosophy, it must be maintained that some philosophy—some underlying set of beliefs about the nature and value of one's field—is absolutely necessary if one is to be effective as a professional and if one's profession is to be effective as a whole. Indeed, one of the most pressing needs of the profession is a statement of philosophy which captures the sense of where the profession stands and where it is going, and which provides a common point of reference from which new and differing ideas can spring. And while the little word "A" in the title of this book indicates that the philosophy to be offered is a *particular* philosophy (it is not, to be very explicit, offered as *The* philosophy of music education) the writer believes that it does indeed capture the self-image of the profession as it is evolving at this point in history. Given the conditions of changing beliefs and differing beliefs, it still remains possible to characterize the general state of beliefs at particular times. There exists at present a surprisingly high level of agreement about the nature of music and music education among those who have given serious thought to this matter. What the profession seems to need at the moment is not persuasion about any particular philosophy, but articulation, refinement, and careful application of the commonly held but largely unarticulated, unrefined, and imperfectly applied beliefs now current.

The need for a philosophy exists at two levels. First, the profession as a whole needs a formulation which can serve to guide the efforts of the group. The impact the profession can make on society depends in large degree on the quality of the profession's understanding of what it has to offer which might be of value to society. There is an almost desperate need for a better understanding of the value of music and of the teaching and learning of music. An uncomfortable amount of defensiveness, of self-doubt, of grasping at straws which seem to offer bits and pieces of self-justification, exists now in music education and has always seemed to exist. It would be difficult to find a field so active, so apparently healthy, so venerable in age and widespread in practice, which is at the same time so worried about its inherent value.

The tremendous expenditure of concern about how to justify itself —both to itself and to others—which has been traditional in this field, reflects a lack of philosophical "inner peace." What a terrible shame this is. For, as will be made clear in this book, justification for teaching and learning music exists at the very deepest levels of human value. Until music education understands what it really has to offer, until it is convinced of the fact that it is a necessary rather than a peripheral part of human culture, until it "feels in its bones" that its value is a fundamental one, it will not have attained the peace of mind which is the mark of maturity. And it also will not have reached a level of operational effectiveness which is an outgrowth of self-acceptance, of security, of purposes understood and efforts channeled.

While a philosophy can serve as a sort of "collective conscience" for music education as a whole, the strength of the field ultimately depends on the convictions of its members. As necessary as a philosophy might be for the over-all effectiveness of a group, it is even more necessary that the individuals who comprise the group have come to an understanding of the nature and the value of their individual endeavors.

This is so for three reasons. First, the individual who has a clear notion of what his aims are as a professional, and who is convinced of the importance of these aims, is a strong link in the chain of people who collectively make a profession. Music education has been fortunate in having leaders who have held strong convictions, who have helped enormously to forge a sense of group identity. But too many convictions have been based on platitudes, on attractive but empty arguments, on vague intimations that music education is important with little in the way of solid reasoning to give backbone to beliefs. So many individuals have enormous dedication to this field but little more to base it on than fond hopes. This is why the profession gives the appearance—a very accurate appearance—of tremendous vitality and purposefulness and goodness of intentions, while at the same time the nagging doubt exists as to whether it all makes much difference. In this situation, individuals who do have convincing justifications for music education, who exhibit in their own lives the inner sense of worth which comes from doing important work in the world, become some of the profession's most prized possessions. To the degree that individual music educators are helped to formulate a compelling philosophy, the profession will become more solid and secure.

The second reason for the importance of strengthening individual beliefs about music education is that the understanding a person has about the value and nature of his profession inevitably effects his understanding of the value and nature of his personal life. To a large extent, a person is what he does in life. If his occupation seems to him an important one, which he holds in respect and through which he can enrich both himself and his society, he cannot help but feel that a large part of his life is important and respectable and enriching. If, on the other hand, a person has the feeling that his work is of doubtful value, that it lacks the respect of people both inside and outside his field, that the contribution he makes through his work is peripheral and inconsequential, he can only feel that much of his life is of equally dubious value.

It is crucial that young people preparing to enter the profession of music education develop an understanding of the importance of their chosen field. Perhaps at no other time in life is the need for self-justification as pressing as when a young person is preparing to take his place as a contributing member of society. For such people there is an almost desperate need for a philosophy which provides a mission and a meaning for their professional lives. This is especially the case when, as in music education, the value of the field is not fully understood by its members, and is perhaps even less understood by professionals in related fields. Given the lack of convincing arguments about the importance of music education, the philosophical insecurity which manifests itself in superficial bases of self-justification, the general defensiveness of music educators toward their colleagues in other aspects of music and education, it is all too clear why so many music education undergraduates are more or less cynical, detached, insecure, defensive.

Two conditions are necessary if this situation is to be reversed. First, a philosophy is needed which offers a convincing basis for valuing music education. Second, systematic attention to the development of a professional philosophy should occur during undergraduate education. Neither condition prevails at present. Seldom is an undergraduate course devoted to a consideration of the reasons underlying the practices of teaching and learning music. This is partly because there is little available material to use in such a course and few college music education teachers feel qualified to make up for the lack of philosophical ammunition. What attention exists comes, if it comes at all, in bits and pieces at the beginnings of various other courses, in which texts are used where part of chapter one is devoted to "the value of music education." Admirable as such statements might be they do not and can not substitute for serious attention to the complex business of developing a consistent, penetrating philosophy. In fact, the perfunctory nature of attention to matters philosophical, both in college courses and by the texts used, which are intended to serve other purposes, reinforces the notion that there are few, if any, good reasons for music education to exist. The smattering of rationales picked up here and there confuse more than they convince, weaken more than they strengthen, discourage more than they inspire.

Students deserve better than this. It is essential for the development of a sense of self-identity and self-respect that college students be given the opportunity to think seriously about their reasons for professional being. And they deserve to be introduced to a philosophy which is more than a protestation of good intentions. College students are far too sophisticated to be satisfied with superficial reasoning, and they are far too involved with life to be able to accept a philosophy which does not grasp their imagination and tap their zeal. The need of youth to feel that life is significant, that actions do matter, that good causes can be served and good influences be felt, can be met more effectively and immediately by a sound philosophy than by any other aspect of their education. The return on the investment made in developing a professional philosophy is extremely high, not only in providing a basis for self-respect, but in channeling the dedication and commitment of young people into a dedication and commitment to music education.

All that has been said about the purposes a philosophy serves for the music educator in training applies as well to the music educator in service. No matter how long one has been a professional the need for self-understanding and self-esteem exists. In some ways these needs become more complex with time, as professional duties, responsibilities, problems, become more complex. For the veteran music educator (and some would argue that surviving the first year of teaching qualifies the music educator as "veteran"), a goal is needed which focuses efforts toward something more satisfying than another concert, more meaningful than another contest, more important than another class, broader than another lesson or meeting or budget or report. All these obligations and pleasures need to head somewhere. They need to be viewed as the necessary carrying out in practice of an end which transcends each of them—which adds to each of one's duties a purpose deep enough and large enough to make all of them truly worthwhile. It becomes progressively more difficult, very often, for the professional to see beyond the increasing number of trees to the forest which includes all of them. Without the larger view, without a continually deepening sense of the inherent value of one's work, it is very easy to begin to operate at the level of daily problems with little regard for their larger context. Inevitably, an erosion of confidence takes place, in which immediate concerns never seem to mean very much. Having lost a sense of purpose, which was perhaps not very strong to begin with, the teacher begins to doubt his value as a professional and as an individual.

The inspiring, rejuvenating, joyful nature of music itself is a strong barrier to loss of concern among those who deal with it professionally. This is one of the major benefits of being a music educator. But fortunate as this is, a set of beliefs which explains very clearly the reasons for music's power remains necessary if the music educator is to function as more than a technician. Too often beliefs about music and arguments for its importance have been at the level of the obvious, with the secret hope that if one justified music education by appeals to easily understood, facile arguments, its "deeper" values would somehow prevail. Just what these deeper values are usually remains a mystery, but they are sensed. So one plugs along, using whatever arguments turn up to bolster oneself in one's own and others' eyes, trusting that all will turn out well in the end. But as time goes along, for the individual and for the profession as a whole, it becomes less and less possible to be sustained by hazy hopes. A time for candor presents itself, when the question can no longer be avoided: "Just what is it about my work that really matters?"

The function of a professional philosophy is to answer that question. A good answer should be developed while a person is preparing to enter the profession. If not, any time is better than no time. If the answer is a good one it will serve to pull together thoughts about the fundamental nature and value of one's professional efforts in a way which allows for these thoughts to grow and change with time and experience. It is not possible for a philosophy to serve such a purpose if the effort to accomplish the fundamental is based on the superficial. A strong philosophy must illuminate the deepest level of values in one's field. At this level one can find not only professional fulfillment, but the personal fulfillment which is an outgrowth of being a secure professional.

The third reason for the importance of a convincing professional philosophy is the fact that everything the music educator does in his job is a carrying out in practice of his beliefs about his subject. However nebulous those beliefs, however disjointed or unarticulated, they are there and they are in operation. Every time a choice is made, a belief is applied. The music teacher, as every other professional, makes hundreds of small and large choices every day, each one based on a decision that one thing rather than another should be done. The quality of these decisions depends directly on the quality of the teacher's understanding of the nature of his subject. The deeper this understanding the more consistent, the more focused, the more effective become the teacher's choices. The teacher who lacks a clear understanding of his subject can only make choices by hunch and by hope, these being a reflection of the state of his beliefs.

Perhaps at no other time in the history of education has there been as unanimous a conviction as at present, that a necessary condition of effective teaching is a clear understanding of the nature of the subject being taught. The educational reform movement which began in the 1950's, which continues unabated to this day, and which is now being joined by the field of music education, has been guided by several concerns, all bearing on the necessity for a philosophy which provides a firm understanding of the nature of one's subject.

The first and perhaps most characteristic of these concerns has been a reaffirmation of the importance of the great disciplines of human thought. Several reasons exist for this turn of events. The Progressive Education movement, which was the basis for educational reform during the period from around 1918 to 1935, laid great emphasis on expanding the role of the school to include more than formal, intellectual learning. Social and recreational activities became an important part of schooling, as did vocational and utilitarian training. While this had the effect of making the school a truer reflection of society and a more influential force in the lives of children, and enormously strengthened the position of music education, it also led to a decline in emphasis on teaching subjects for their inherent value. Quite contrary to the position of John

Dewey, the most important founder of Progressive Education, school practices shifted somewhat from academic learning to social adjustment.[1]

After the mid-1930's, Progressive Education went into decline, and until the 1950's no strong reform movement took place in American Education. Then, in 1957, Sputnik violated the virgin skies, signalling an end to American complacency and an upheaval in American education. Academic scholars, who had paid little attention to the schools, in that they found them for the most part to be irrelevant, now mounted an attack on the educational "establishment." They decried the concern for "life adjustment" and the lack of academic rigor, these being the least desirable but perhaps most visible remnants of Progressive Education. The entry of subject matter scholars into the debate about education, the need for immediate gains in the quality of teaching and learning, especially in the sciences, the dramatic realization of the strategic and pervasive role of schooling in developing a secure society, all set off shock waves still being felt in every area of educational thought and practice.[2]

While the first reform efforts were directed quite naturally toward quick improvements in the teaching of mathematics and the physical sciences, the perspective of time has broadened the views of what high quality education should be. A new emphasis has emerged on the primacy of genuine understanding about the nature of the major disciplines of knowledge. While this is partly a reaction to Progressive Education and a reflection of immediate national needs, it has also become a recognition that if the quality of life in a terribly complex society is to be more than superficial, learning must be more than superficial. The major disciplines are major because they are the basic ways available

---

[1] Paul Woodring, "Reform Movements from the Point of View of Psychological Theory," in *Theories of Learning and Instruction,* ed. Ernest R. Hilgard, The Sixty-third Yearbook of the National Society for the Study of Education, Part I (Chicago: The University of Chicago Press, 1964), pp. 286–290. For a definitive account of the rise and fall of Progressive Education, see Lawrence A. Cremin, *The Transformation of the School* (New York: Alfred A. Knopf, Inc., 1961).

[2] For histories and descriptions of educational reform and particular curriculum projects, see John I. Goodlad, *School Curriculum Reform in the United States* (New York: The Fund for the Advancement of Education, 477 Madison Avenue, 1964) and the many publications of the Association for Supervision and Curriculum Development, NEA Building, 1201 Sixteenth Street, N.W., Washington, D.C. 20036. Applications of specific curriculum reform principles to music education have been made by the author in "The Curriculum Reform Explosion and the Problem of Secondary General Music," *Music Educators Journal,* LII, No. 3 (January, 1966) and "Curriculum Reform and the Junior High General Music Class," *Music Educators Journal,* LIII, No. 2 (October, 1966). For a description of several curriculum reform projects in music education, see the author's "New Curriculum Developments in Music Education," in *Influences in Curriculum Change,* ed. Gladys G. Unruh and Robert R. Leeper (Washington, D.C., Association for Supervision and Curriculum Development, 1968).

to human beings to know about themselves and their world. Education should help every individual understand the nature, or "structure," of the great disciplines, because the quality of this knowledge determines the quality of a person's understanding of his life and of his environment. Why should every person be given the opportunity to understand the nature of mathematics? Because mathematics is a basic way of "knowing" about reality. Why should every person be given the opportunity to understand the nature of language? Because language, again, is a basic way for humans to "know" about reality. Why should every person be given the opportunity to understand the nature of physics, of chemistry, of geography, of history? Because all of these are basic ways for human beings to understand the nature of the real.

And now, with great courage, with great relief, with great hopes, those concerned with the arts in education can ask the same question and give the same answer. Why should every person be given the opportunity to understand the nature of the art of music? Because the art of music is a basic way of "knowing" about reality.

This single idea has the power to transform the teaching and learning of music in American education. At one stroke it affirms the art of music as one of the great disciplines of human thought, establishes the value of music education as being at the same level as the value of all important education, prescribes the direction that music education must take if it is to fulfill its present mission, rids the profession of any need or desire to depend on outworn rationales for being, and provides the hope that music education will play a far more important role for society in the future than it has in the past.

The task of a philosophy is to explain the meaning of all these claims. If music education is to fulfill the claims it must understand them and know how to apply them. The individual music teacher must know what they mean and how they affect teaching and learning in music. The statement made earlier, that "everything the music educator does in his job is a carrying out in practice of his beliefs about his subject," can now be understood with more clarity. If the job of music education is to help all children understand the nature of the art of music, so they can share the insights into reality which music contains, the music teacher must himself understand the nature of music and must teach in a way which is true to this nature.

It is a shocking fact that the nature and value of music are not understood by many who teach it. Inevitably, this makes much of music education unmusical in nature and in value. But disturbing as this is, music education is far from being alone in realizing that too much of what it has been doing has been beside the point. It was precisely this realization that led to the present reform movement in American education. As each subject matter field began to examine its status in education it found that the subject as it was being taught in school had too little to do with the subject as it actually existed outside of educational settings. School mathematics was quite a different thing from mathematics as practiced by experts in the field. School physics bore little resemblance to physics as understood by competent physicists. Language as taught in school was often quite unlike the way language was used in reality. In subject after subject this gap was found to exist. It would not be inaccurate to describe educational reform in our times as consisting primarily of a closing of gaps between subjects as taught in school and the essential nature of the subjects as understood by those who use and know the subjects best.

Music education is displaying the same concern as every other subject to become true to its nature. It is clear that much of music education has been only marginally musical, and that this has alienated competent musicians and musical scholars, who for a long period of time have regarded school music as being of little if any real value. Certainly music education could have benefitted from the help and sympathy of composers, performers, scholars, but saying this is indulging in hindsight. *Every* subject could say the same about its non-education professionals. That practicing musicians have begun to become concerned about music education, that their initial disdain is turning into positive help, that music educators are becoming less worried about defending past practices and more willing to capitalize on and add to what they do well, that a new spirit of cooperation is emerging based on the dawning realization that music education is the property of *everyone* interested in music—all this is evidence that music has entered the mainstream of educational reform.

In the perspective of these events the usefulness of a philosophy of music education should be evident. If music education is to become *music* education, and if at the same time it is to be *aesthetic* education, it must proceed from a clear understanding of the aesthetic nature and aesthetic value of music. If it was ever true that "theory" was unrelated to "practice," it certainly is true no longer. And it is not only in the field of education that practice and theory have become interdependent. In medicine, in engineering, in chemistry, in biology, in theology, in politics, in every major area of human endeavor, theory and practice can be viewed as two necessary dimensions of the same phenomenon.

The "practicality" of a philosophy of music education extends to every corner of the music education enterprise. Most obviously, a philosophy stipulates the most important objectives of music education. Without the ordering of values which a philosophy supplies, specifying objectives in music education becomes a matter of drawing up long lists of behaviors. It is the function of a philosophy to provide broad objectives under which specific behaviors and behavior-clusters can be chosen intelligently and influenced effectively. Without the synthesizing, directing force of a philosophy, education can only be indiscriminate and diffuse. Every aspect of the teaching and learning of music is similarly influenced by a philosophy. If problems of method, of program, of organization and administration, of evaluation, even of research, are to be dealt with in ways which are relevant to the nature and value of music education, that nature and value must be clearly understood. A philosophy, then, provides the foundation on which the entire structure of music education rests.

QUESTIONS FOR DISCUSSION

1. The philosophy offered in this book is based on an investigation of the nature and value of music. What might be some other bases for a music education philosophy? What strengths and weaknesses exist for each?

2. If it is true that philosophies keep changing, why should one bother to formulate a philosophy at any one time in the history of music education? Why should one bother to formulate a philosophy at any one time in one's own professional life?

3. Why has music education been so insecure about its value? What effect might this insecurity have had on actual music education practices in schools and colleges?

4. Do you know any music educators who seem to have a deep, inner conviction about the importance of their profession? How is their conviction manifested in their behavior?

5. Do you know any music educators who seem to lack a sense of conviction about the importance of their profession? How is their lack of conviction manifested in their behavior?

6. Do undergraduates in other fields of music or in other subjects seem to have a higher level of professional self-respect than those in music education? Explain your answer.

7. Why might a solid philosophy help one maintain a high level of dedication to one's work?

8. What are some actual choices a music teacher must make day by day which reflect, consciously or unconsciously, his professional philosophy?

CHAPTER TWO

alternative views about art on which a philosophy can be based

In the long, tortuous history of aesthetics thousands of views have been expressed about art. To one who examines these views with any degree of objectivity it becomes evident that here, if no place else, is a perfect example of truth being relative. So strong is this impression, so overwhelming its effect, that one is tempted to throw up his hands in despair, turn his back on the entire field of aesthetics, and proclaim that in aesthetic education one might as well do whatever strikes his fancy, since there probably exists plenty of justification for whatever this happens to be.

To yield to this temptation, however, is to give oneself up to ineffectuality. Of course there is no immutable truth in aesthetics. Of course there is no single or simple answer to every question. Of course there is no one guideline which will insure satisfactory results of action. The question is, can one accept this condition and at the same time develop a point of view which helps one's efforts to be as consistent, as effective, as useful for one's purposes as intelligence and modesty allow?

There is really no alternative but to answer "yes." Everything we do in this world is done in the face of imperfect and partial knowledge.

But it is possible—in fact, it is necessary—to adopt some working premises and to use them (not be used *by* them) as guidelines to action, knowing full well that they may be altered or even dropped as conditions change. To refuse to work from a critically accepted position about the nature of one's subject is to avoid one of the central imperatives of human life, which is to carve out, from all existing possibilities, the most reasonable possibilities for one's purposes. Not to do so dooms one to intellectual and operational paralysis. To do so blindly and irrevocably insures the same fate. Searching out a convincing, useful, coherent point of view, adopting it as a base of operations, examining it and sharpening it and tightening it while using it, opening it to new ideas and altering it as seems necessary, can help one to act with purpose, with impact, with some measure of meaningfulness.

The problem, of course, is to determine the best possible point of view. Several principles can help us do so. First, the field of aesthetics must be approached in a highly selective way. It would be beside the point (and quite impossible) to investigate indiscriminately the writings of every aesthetician in history, or every aesthetician of this century, or every aesthetician alive today, looking for leads to a philosophy of music education. Instead, the search must start with an acquaintance with the field of music education; its problems, its needs, its history, its present status. Aesthetics must be used by the music educator to serve his purposes. Otherwise he is likely to lose himself in the history and problems of aesthetics, never to emerge with a workable philosophy. A philosophy should articulate a consistent and helpful statement about the nature and value of music and music education. Only those portions of aesthetics useful for this purpose need be used.

Second, the point of view adopted should be sufficiently broad to take into account all major aspects of music and music education, but sufficiently focused to provide tangible guidelines for thought and action. No single aesthetician has supplied the breadth of conception needed for our purpose, although, as will be seen, some have been of unusual help. It will be necessary to identify an aesthetic position which includes major thinkers and which at the same time has an identifiable structure of ideas which can be handled without being overwhelming in complexity.

Third, the point of view should be particularly pertinent to the art of music, but at the same time capable of yielding insights into the nature of all the arts. Some aesthetic theories are heavily slanted toward the non-musical arts, and while they offer insights into music they do so only secondarily. An example would be the psychoanalytic theory of Carl G. Jung, which is immensely fruitful of ideas about literature, poetry and the visual arts, but which has little to say about music. (2, pp. 140–54; 1, pp. 347–48).*[1] Obviously this situation should be reversed for our purposes, although a view confined to a single art, even music, would be unacceptable also.

Fourth, the view being sought must contain rich implications for education. It would be of little use to adopt a theory which offered few leads to teaching and learning music and the other arts, no matter how strong the theory might be in other matters. Existentialist aesthetics, for example, has provided powerful insights into the nature of art and its role in human life. (1, pp. 363–76).[2] But helpful as these insights are, they do not seem to lend themselves directly or abundantly to problems of mass education. It would be difficult, therefore, to depend on this particular view for a philosophy of music education.

Finally, any aesthetic position to be used as a basis for a philosophy must be relevant to the society in which we live and to the general conditions under which American education operates. Important as Marxism-Leninism has been in history, for example (1, pp. 355–63) it is quite peripheral to our concerns. The same can be said about Freudian aesthetics and Oriental aesthetics and Medieval aesthetics. All of these, and others, can be of use for particular purposes, but they can not be the foundation on which our philosophy is to be built.

Of all existing aesthetic viewpoints,[3] one in particular fulfills the principles outlined above and does so with unusual power. This view is presented by Leonard B. Meyer (7) as one of three related aesthetic theories; Absolute Formalism, Absolute Expressionism and Referentialism. An explanation of each of these theories will set the stage for the choice to be made as to which will best serve as the basis for a philosophy, and for our systematic examination of the implications of using this theory as a base of operations.

The words "Absolutism" and "Referentialism" tell one where to go to find the meaning and value of a work of art. The Absolutist says that in order to find an art work's meaning, you must go to the work itself and attend to the qualities which make the work a created thing. In

---

* References in parentheses refer to the Supplementary Readings at the ends of the chapters in this book.

[1] An excellent introduction to the monumental work of Jung is Carl G. Jung, ed., *Man and his Symbols* (Garden City, New York: Doubleday & Company, Inc., 1964).

[2] Also see Arturo B. Fallico, *Art and Existentialism* (Englewood Cliffs, N.J.: Prentice-Hall, Inc., 1962).

[3] All the major "isms" in aesthetics are reviewed in Monroe C. Beardsley, *Aesthetics* (New York: The Macmillan Company, 1966).

music, you would go to the sounds themselves, and attend to what those sounds do.

The Referentialist disagrees. According to his view, the meaning and value of a work of art exist outside of the work itself. In order to find the art work's meaning you must go to the ideas, emotions, attitudes, events, which the work *refers* you to in the world outside the art work. The function of the art work is to remind you of, or tell you about, or help you understand, or make you experience, something which is extra-artistic; that is, something which is outside the created thing and the artistic qualities which make it a created thing. In music, the sounds should serve as a reminder of, or a clue to, or a sign of something extra-musical; something separate from the sounds and what the sounds are doing. To the degree that the music is successful in referring you to a non-musical experience it is a successful piece of music. To the degree that the experience is an important or valuable one the music is itself important or valuable.

The most clear-cut example of Referentialism is the Communist theory of art, called "Socialist Realism." This view, which is the official aesthetic doctrine of Marxism-Leninism, regards art as a servant of social and political needs. The function of art is to further the cause of the state by influencing attitudes toward social problems and by illuminating the needs of the state and the proper actions to be taken to fulfill those needs. As stated in the Statute of the Union of Soviet Writers:

> Socialist Realism is the fundamental method of Soviet Litera-ture and criticism [and of all art]: it demands of the artist a true, historically concrete representation of reality in its revo-lutionary development. Further, it ought to contribute to the ideological transformation and education of the workers in the spirit of socialism.[4]

According to Socialist Realism, and for any referential theory of art, the key factor of value is the non-aesthetic goodness of the art work's "message." If a particular art work has no identifiable, non-artistic message (a piece of "pure" instrumental music, for example), it must be regarded as merely a titillation of the senses with no value beyond that of sheer decoration. Of course any message in the art work must be presented attractively, but the artistic attractiveness only serves to make the message more vivid, more powerfully felt. To the extent that artistic interest becomes the central value of the work and non-artistic aspects are diminished in importance, the work is decadent and useless.

---

[4] Beardsley, *Aesthetics*, p. 360.

The message in an art work, according to Referentialism, need not be an intellectual or practical one: it can also be an "emotional" one. If a work makes people feel a particular, desirable, useful emotion, it would fulfill the conditions for "good" art. The emotion must be identifiable; it must be unambiguous and concrete, and it must be the kind which serves some non-artistic end, such as closer identification with fellow workers, or higher regard for the community, or deeper sympathy for those less fortunate, etc. If the emotion in a work is not of this specific, non-artistically directed kind; if it is, instead, an integral and inseparable part of the artistic qualities in the work and is therefore experienced as an ineffable sense of feeling, the work is to that extent, again, decadent and useless.

The notion that art works arouse non-artistic emotions and that one must carefully choose which of these emotions *should* be aroused is as old as Plato, who felt that the kinds of music used by the general public should be severely limited so that their moral fiber would not be weakened through the effects of hearing voluptuous tunes. The strongest statement of this position in modern times is that of Leo Tolstoy. It will repay us to take a brief look at Tolstoy's views, in making very explicit the consequences of taking a thoroughgoing referentialist viewpoint.

For Tolstoy, the function of art is to transmit specific emotions from the artist to the recipient in the most direct and most powerful way the artist can devise. If the artist can transmit an emotion which is individual; that is, which is a particular, precise, concrete emotion: if the emotion is transmitted clearly and unambiguously, so there is no question about what the recipient should feel: and if the artist sincerely feels the emotion himself and has the need to express it, the work of art is likely to be a good one. (4, pp. 140–41). All these principles illustrate the emotional dimension of Referentialism.

But in addition to transmitting a specific emotion and doing it well, the quality of the art work also depends on the desirability of the particular emotion transmitted. If it is a "bad" emotion the art work will be pernicious in its effects. If it is a "good" emotion the art work will be beneficent in its effects. So, inevitably, for Tolstoy and for any referentialist, one must judge a work of art on the basis of its non-artistic subject matter—its content of reference to the world which is outside the work and which is separate from the work's artistic qualities. One can specify good and bad emotions according to one's view of what is good and what is bad in life. According to Tolstoy, good emotions are those which lead toward Christian brotherhood. Unfortunately, very few art works fulfill his criteria of goodness. "In modern painting, strange to say, works of this kind, directly transmitting the Christian feeling of love of God and of one's neighbor are hardly to be found, especially among the works of the celebrated painters."[5]

Tolstoy finds very few art works in any medium that satisfy his demands for good art, although occasionally a few crop up—*Uncle Tom's Cabin,* Millet's "The Man with the Hoe," china dolls and other ornaments which are easily comprehensible to everyone, etc. In music his position is illustrated most strikingly. The best examples of music are marches and dances, which approach the condition of having a distinct, easily understood message. The popular songs of the various nations are also great art, but in "learned" music there are precious few examples from which to choose—the Violin Aria by Bach, the E-flat Major Nocturne of Chopin, some scattered selections from Haydn, Mozart, Schubert. Beethoven is perhaps the poorest of composers and the weakest of his compositions is the Ninth Symphony. This is so because

> not only do I not see how the feelings transmitted by this work
> could unite people not specially trained to submit themselves
> to its complex hypnotism, but I am unable to imagine to myself
> a crowd of normal people who could understand anything of
> this long, confused, and artificial production, except short
> snatches which are lost in a sea of what is incomprehensible.
> And therefore, whether I like it or not, I am compelled to con-
> clude that this work belongs to the rank of bad art.[6]

But Beethoven is in good company, for in the same classification (along with paintings which display "all that odious female nudity")[7]

> belongs almost all the chamber and opera music of our times,
> beginning especially from Beethoven (Schumann, Berlioz,
> Liszt, Wagner), by its subject matter devoted to the expression
> of feelings accessible only to people who have developed in
> themselves an unhealthy, nervous irritation evoked by this ex-
> clusive, artificial, and complex music.[8]

The reason for dwelling a bit on Tolstoy's aesthetic views is that they present the most thorough statement of Referentialism available, and can serve as a foil against which the other views to be presented can

---

5 Leo N. Tolstoy, *What Is Art?,* trans. Aylmer Maude (Indianapolis: The Liberal Arts Press, Inc., 1960), p. 152. Reprinted by permission of The Liberal Arts Press Division of The Bobbs-Merrill Company, Inc.

6 Tolstoy, *What Is Art?,* p. 158.

7 Tolstoy, *What Is Art?,* p. 153.

8 Tolstoy, *What Is Art?,* p. 157.

be compared. Another very obvious example of Referentialism should be noted, this one in musical aesthetics, because it also will help keep straight the three viewpoints to be explained here. This is the view of the English aesthetician Deryck Cooke. (3).

Mr. Cooke is in agreement with Tolstoy that music is by nature a language and that, as with any good language, the meaning of the terms used in the language can be specified. This notion will be explored in several places throughout this book, so no explanation will be made at this point. It need only be noted that the conception of art as "language" (by which is meant a system of symbols having conventional referents) is a purely referential one and leads inevitably to a search for the proper "meanings" of the language's terms. While Cooke recognizes the difficulty of stipulating precise referents for musical "language terms," the difficulty, according to him, can be overcome by intellectual effort. As a step in this direction he analyzes the notes of the major, minor and chromatic scales, and several basic melodic patterns, to find the emotional referent of each. To the extent that he succeeds in doing so, according to his theory, he succeeds in revealing the meanings hidden in the musical sounds. The task, obviously, is one of translation; of "breaking the code" so to speak. (3, p. 34).

After long analyses of the use of various intervals and note patterns, Mr. Cooke offers his conclusions as to their referents. A selection of these follows:

Minor Second: . . . spiritless anguish, context of finality.
Minor Third: . . . stoic acceptance, tragedy.
Major Third: . . . joy.
Sharp Fourth: . . . devilish and inimical forces.
Major Seventh: . . . violent longing, aspiration in a context of finality.
Ascending 1-(2)-3-(4)-5 (major): . . . an outgoing, active, assertive emotion of joy.
Ascending 1-(2)-3-(4)-5 (minor): . . . an outgoing feeling of pain—an assertion of sorrow, a complaint, a protest against misfortune.
Descending 5-(4)-3-(2)-1 (minor): . . . an "incoming" painful emotion, in a context of finality: acceptance of, or yielding to grief: discouragement and depression; passive suffering; and the despair connected with death.[9]

---

[9] Deryck Cooke, *The Language of Music* (London, Oxford University Press, 1959), pp. 90, 115, 122, 133. Quotations reprinted by permission of Oxford University Press.

The use of these translations by the knowledgable listener should allow, according to Cooke, for full participation in music's meaning. Is this oversimplifying the case? Not according to Cooke, for

> Actually, the process of musical communication is fundamentally a very simple one, which only appears complicated because of its complicated apparatus. There is nothing more involved about it than there is in any form of emotional expression—say, a physical movement or a vocal utterance.[10]

Beethoven's music, for example, would not be needed if Beethoven could personally communicate his inner joy by jumping or shouting in the presence of an audience. To convert his emotion into permanent form he used sounds, so that many people, even after his death, could experience with him the joy that he felt. (3, p. 209). Music, then, is essentially a giving vent to emotions through sounds.

While the examples of Referentialism given here are obviously extreme ones, many opinions about and practices in aesthetic education share some of the same assumptions, even if not as consistently or strongly. For example, the idea that when non-aesthetic subject matter exists in a work of art (fruit in a painting, political theories in a novel, a story or "program" in music) the art work is "about" that subject matter, is a referentialist assumption. If one isolates the subject matter; say, the story of *Til Eulenspiegel,* and teaches about it as if the story was what the music is about, one is acting as a Referentialist. If one adds a story or message to an art work which contains none; say, Mozart's *Eine kleine Nachtmusik,* one is, again, acting as a Referentialist. The same applies to "emotional" content. Teaching about love and its meaning as the content of the *Liebestod,* or identifying the content of Beethoven's Funeral March as "sadness," and teaching about sadness and its roots, its implications, etc., are practices compatible with Referentialism.

Music educators and others concerned with the arts in the schools will recognize that referentialist assumptions are in operation in much that is done in the teaching of art. The isolating of and teaching about the meaning of the words in vocal music; the same process in program music; the searching out of a "message" in absolute music; the attempt to add a story or picture to music, either verbally or visually; the search for the right emotion-words with which to characterize music; the comparing of musical works with works in other art forms according to similarities in subject matter; these and many other practices attest to the presence of Referentialism in music education.

---

[10] Cooke, *The Language of Music,* p. 209.

What is the value of art, according to the referentialist point of view? Obviously, the values of art and of being involved with art are non-artistic values. Art works serve many purposes, all of them extra-aesthetic. If one can share these values one becomes a better citizen, a better worker, a better human being, to the extent that art influences one in non-artistic ways and these influences are assumed to be beneficial. Of course, there is the danger that harmful works of art will have harmful effects, so care must be taken in the choice of art works. This is why societies which operate under a referentialist aesthetic must exercise a high degree of control over the artistic diet of their citizens. Teachers, if they are Referentialists, are in the position of having to make decisions as to which art works are proper for their students and which improper, these judgments being based on the non-artistic effects of the art works' subject matter.

As with teaching practices based on Referentialism, music educators will have no difficulty recognizing the referentialist basis for many of the value claims made for music education. Studying music makes one a better person in many ways: it improves learning skills; it imparts moral uplift; it fulfills a wide variety of social needs; it provides a healthy outlet for repressed emotions; it encourages self-discipline; it provides a challenge to focus efforts upon; it gives a basis for worthy use of leisure time; it improves health in countless ways; it is assumed to be, in short, a most effective way to make people better people—non-aesthetically.

Let us return now to the aesthetic point of view called Absolutism. It will be recalled that this view asserts that the meaning and value of a work of art are to be found in the qualities which make the work a created thing—the very qualities which the Referentialist insists are only the bearers of meanings *outside* themselves. In music, according to Absolutism, the sounds and what they do are inherently meaningful, and if one is to share their "meaning" one must attend to the sounds and not to anything the sounds might remind one of in the extra-aesthetic realm outside the music.

At the opposite end of the aesthetic spectrum from the Referentialist is the Absolutist who is also a Formalist. The Absolute Formalist asserts that the "meaning" of an art work is like no other meaning in all the experience of man. Aesthetic events, such as sounds in music, mean *only themselves:* the meaning is *sui generis,* completely and essentially different from anything in the world which is non-musical:

> . . . to appreciate a work of art we need bring with us nothing
> from life, no knowledge of its ideas and affairs, no familiarity
> with its emotions. Art transports us from the world of man's
> activity to a world of aesthetic exaltation. For a moment we

are shut off from human interests; our anticipations and memories are arrested; we are lifted above the stream of life.[11]

The experience of art, for the Formalist, is primarily an intellectual one; it is the recognition and appreciation of form for its own sake. This recognition and appreciation, while intellectual in character, is called by Formalists an "emotion"—usually, the "aesthetic emotion." But this so-called "emotion" is a unique one—it has no counterpart in other emotional experiences:

> . . . he who contemplates a work of art, inhabit(s) a world with an intense and peculiar significance of its own; that significance is unrelated to the significance of life. In this world the emotions of life find no place. It is a world with emotions of its own.[12]

The Formalist does not deny that many art works contain references to the world outside the work. But he insists that all such references are *totally irrelevant* to the art work's meaning:

> . . . no one who has a real understanding of the art of painting attaches any importance to what we call the subject of a picture—what is represented . . . all depends on *how* it is presented, *nothing* on what. Rembrandt expressed his profoundest feelings just as well when he painted a carcass hanging up in a butcher's shop as when he painted the Crucifixion or his mistress.[13]

In music, since it is capable of being entirely untainted with non-aesthetic subject matter, the Formalist finds the clearest example of artistic meaning. In a complete reversal of Referentialism, the Formalist claims that "Definite feelings and emotions are unsusceptible of being embodied in music."[14] Instead, "The ideas which a composer expresses are mainly and primarily of a purely musical nature."[15] There is no correspondence whatsoever between the beauty we find in the non-artistic

---

11 Clive Bell, *Art* (New York: G. P. Putnam's Sons, 1914), p. 25. Quotations reprinted by permission of Putnam's, Professor Quentin Bell and Chatto & Windus Ltd., London.

12 Bell, *Art*, pp. 26, 27.

13 Roger Fry, *The Artist and Psycho-Analysis*, Hogarth Essays (London: Hogarth Press, 1924), p. 308. Reprinted by permission of Mrs. Pamela Diamand and the Hogarth Press.

14 Eduard Hanslick, *The Beautiful in Music*, trans. Gustav Cohen (Indianapolis: The Liberal Arts Press, Inc., 1957), p. 21. Reprinted by permission of The Liberal Arts Press Division of The Bobbs-Merrill Company, Inc.

15 Hanslick, *The Beautiful in Music*, p. 23.

world and the beauty we find in art, for art's beauty is a separate kind. This is especially the case in music, in which the nature of the beautiful ". . . is specifically musical. By this we mean that the beautiful is not contingent upon nor in need of any subject introduced from without, but that it consists wholly of sounds artistically combined."[16]

Unfortunately, it is given to few people to be able to enjoy the peculiar, special, esoteric kind of experience which the contemplation of formal relationships offers. According to the Formalist, most people, being inherently incapable of pure aesthetic enjoyment, satisfy themselves with non-aesthetic reactions to art works; that is, with reactions to the referents of the works. This completely misses the point of art, of course, but the Formalist assumes that this is to be expected. Given the special nature of the aesthetic and the general insensitivity of most people, we should not be too concerned if art's value is available on only a limited basis, and we should not have any illusions that most people will ever understand that the real value of art is quite different from what they think it is.

The further removed from the events and objects of life, the purer the appeal to the intellect which can apprehend fine distinctions in formal relations, the more exquisite the arrangement of aesthetic properties, the freer from ordinary emotions not directly dependent on form, the better the art work and the more aesthetic the experience of it. In the rarified realm of pure form, untouched by the homeliness of ordinary life, the Formalist finds his satisfaction and his delight. He does not expect to find much company there.

Pure Formalism, as pure Referentialism, represents an extreme view of the nature and value of art. However, as some beliefs and practices in aesthetic education are based on assumptions of Referentialism, many are based on Formalist suppositions. The practice of isolating the formal elements of art works and studying them for their own sake is the counterpart of separating out the referential elements. The study of art as a "discipline," with primary attention given to the accumulation of information or the development of skills, is formalistic in flavor. That the major value of music education is intellectual; that the study of "the fundamentals" is, in and of itself, a beneficial thing; that musical experience consists primarily of using the mind to ferret out all possible tonal relationships; that music, or art in general, transports one from the real world into the ethereal world of the aesthetic; all these are assumptions compatible with Formalism.

Perhaps the most widespread application of Formalism to music

---

[16] Hanslick, *The Beautiful in Music*, p. 47.

education is the policy of teaching the talented and entertaining the remaining masses. Music education in recent history has focused major effort on developing the musical skills of children with talent, and in this it has achieved a high level of success. And why, after all, should one worry about the general population, which is never going to be aesthetically educated anyhow? As with all special abilities, artistic enjoyment is possible for a few, and these are the ones who can benefit from serious music education. As for music in general education, let it be pleasant, let it be attractive, let it be amusing, but don't expect authentic musical learning to take place. Teachers who care to devote themselves to music education for the masses, whether through missionary zeal or lack of musical ability, are certainly welcome to do so, but they should not expect to be regarded with the same respect as those who are engaged in serious music teaching. It is not surprising, given the pervasiveness of this formalistic view, however subliminal it might be, that music education has achieved so much in the performance program and so little in the general music program. It is also not surprising, in view of the educational reform movement in our times, that the entire profession has become alarmed over this situation and determined to improve upon it.

While Referentialism and Formalism are contradictory in the major aspects of their theories, both contain a measure of truth. One can agree with the Referentialist that art works are affected by their subject matter. One can also agree that art and feelings are intimately connected. Perhaps it is so that art can serve non-artistic ends. But how are these ideas reconciled with the equally convincing ideas that art works can be entirely devoid of subject matter and in any case always transcend subject matter; that aesthetic reactions are not identical to ordinary emotions; that art's value is inherently aesthetic rather than non-aesthetic?

When considering each of these two viewpoints separately it is difficult (perhaps impossible) to give full assent to either. There is no evidence to support the Referentialist's claim that artists or art lovers are better citizens, behave more morally, are more socially adjusted, are healthier, etc. The use of art as propaganda—no matter whether for good or bad causes—perverts the nature of the artistic impulse. To translate the "meaning" of art into non-artistic terms, whether cognitive or emotional, is to violate the meaningfulness of aesthetic experience. And to justify the arts in education on the basis of values least characteristic of art is to miss the point of what art really does have to offer.

At the same time it is not possible to regard art, with the Formalist, as an intellectual exercise. Surely art is intimately connected to life rather than totally distinct from it. The sense of significance we get from art is a sense applicable to the significance of human life, and the beauty or truth we find in art has some relation to the beauty or truth of life as lived and known. To assume that art is a fragile thing, suitable for some people but irrelevant for most, and that education should reflect this exclusiveness, disregards the power and pervasiveness of art in human life and the obligation of education to share life's goods fully.

So while each view contains some truth, each also contains major falsehoods which prevent their use as a basis for a philosophy. Somehow their contributions to understanding must be preserved while their limitations are overcome.

This brings us to a third aesthetic theory, Absolute Expressionism, which, it will be argued in this book, does in fact include the elements of truth found in both Referentialism and Formalism. But Expressionism is not in any sense a combination of the other two. It is a distinctive, coherent viewpoint, requiring systematic explanation if its major tenets are to be understood. These tenets, it is believed, will be found to be as widely acceptable by aestheticians, artists and educators as any available in aesthetic theory. Further, the views of Absolute Expressionism seem to be most suitable to mass education in a democratic society; most true to the nature of art, as art is conceived in our times; and most germinal of guidelines for teaching and learning music and the other arts in all aspects of educational programs.

The remainder of this book will be devoted to an explanation of Expressionism and its application to music education. A brief overview at this point will introduce the major issues which need to be explored.

First, and most basic, is the clear distinction between Absolutism and Referentialism. The Absolute Expressionist agrees with the Absolute Formalist that the meaning and value of art are to be found in the aesthetic qualities of art works. In this there is an irreconcilable conflict with the referentialist view of art's meaning as a function of subject matter. But while Expressionism cannot accept non-artistic meaning as central to art, it also cannot accept the formalist notion of the intellectual, removed-from-life nature of aesthetic experience. How can it be maintained that the experience of art is *aesthetic* experience, that art's meaning is *aesthetic* meaning, that art's value is *aesthetic* value, and at the same time claim that art can exert a strong effect on the quality of human life? This is the key question, for it states the two conditions which must be met if an aesthetic theory is to be both convincing and useful. First, the nature of art as art must be affirmed. Second, the relation of art to life must be recognized.

The answer to this question has been given in many different ways by many different writers on art. A summary of their views might be stated as follows: the aesthetic components in a work of art are similar in quality to the quality inherent in all human experience. When one shares the qualities contained in an art work's aesthetic content, one is also sharing in the qualities of which all human experience is made. The relation between the qualities of the art work and the qualities of human experience is felt by the perceiver of the work as "significance." To the degree that an art work contains aesthetic qualities which are convincing, vital, keen, and to the degree that these qualities can be experienced by the perceiver the significance of the experience—the relation of the aesthetic qualities to the qualities of life—will be convincing, vital, keen. The residue of sharing the significant aesthetic qualities of the art work is a deeper sense of the nature of human life.

Many words have been used in aesthetics to explain this notion. The following is a summary of the more common ones:

Art:

is expressive of	subjective reality
is analogous to	the quality of experience
is isomorphic with	the emotive life
corresponds to	the patterns of feeling
is a counterpart of	the life of feeling
has the same patterns as	sentience
is a semblance of	the depth of existence
gives images of	the human personality
gives insights into	the realm of affect
gives experience of	the patterns of consciousness
gives understanding of	the significance of experience
gives revelations of	
brings to consciousness	
makes conceivable	

All these terms convey the same sense; that the experience of art is related to the experience of life at the deepest levels of life's significance. One can share the insights of art not by going outside of art to non-artistic references, *but by going deeper into the aesthetic qualities the art work contains.* It is in the aesthetic content of the art work that insights can be found, and the deeper the experience of the aesthetic qualities the deeper can be the sense of significance gained. If the experience of art is to be significant for life, the experience of art must be aesthetic experience.

What is the value of such experience? If it is true that experiences of art yield insights into human subjective reality, the arts may be conceived as a means to self-understanding, a way by which a human's sense of his nature can be explored, clarified, grasped. Many words have been used to describe the value of insight into one's nature as a responsive organism: "self-unification" (John Dewey); "personal identity" (Susanne K. Langer); "individualization" (Leonard B. Meyer); "individuation" (Carl G. Jung); "self-actualization" (Abraham H. Maslow); "integration of the personality" (Paul Tillich). All these terms signify the humanising value of self-knowledge. There are few deeper values than this. And the arts are one of the most effective means known to man to realize this value.

All these statements must be explained and their relevance to music education shown. In what follows, the meaning of Expressionism will be explored as it is manifested in the most important areas of aesthetics: the relation of art and feeling; the process of aesthetic creation; the complex but central problem of aesthetic meaning; and the content of aesthetic experience. This will be followed by a discussion of the particular nature of the art of music. At that point, the implicit and explicit references made throughout the book to education will be applied to the three major aspects of the music education program; general music, performance, and music among the other arts.

QUESTIONS FOR DISCUSSION

1. Why would it be dangerous to start with the field of aesthetics and try to work out a philosophy of music education on the basis of what aesthetics suggests? What role can aesthetics play in the formation of a philosophy?

2. According to Referentialism, where does one find the value of art? Give examples. How would one teach art in order to help people find its referential value? Give examples.

3. According to Formalism, where does one find the value of art? Give examples. How would one teach art for its formal values? Give examples.

4. What seems true and what seems false about Referentialism and about Formalism? Can one be both a Referentialist and a Formalist at the same time?

5. What are some practices in music education other than those mentioned in this chapter which seem to be based on 1) Referentialist assumptions, 2) Formalist assumptions?

6. Can you think of terms other than the ones suggested in this chapter which state the same idea that art (is expressive of) (the realm of human feeling)?

SUPPLEMENTARY READINGS

A. General writings on aesthetics

    1. Beardsley, Monroe C., *Aesthetics*. New York: The Macmillan Company, 1966. This is a most useful history of aesthetics, comprehensive but succinct.

    2. Rader, Melvin, ed., *A Modern Book of Esthetics*. New York: Holt, Rinehart & Winston, Inc., 1962. Perhaps the most widely used collection of essays on the main topics in aesthetics.

B. Referentialism

    3. Cooke, Deryck, *The Language of Music*. London: Oxford University Press, 1959.

    4. Tolstoy, Leo N., *What Is Art?*, trans. Aylmer Maude. Indianapolis: The Liberal Arts Press, Inc., 1960.

C. Formalism

    5. Bell, Clive, *Art*. New York: G. P. Putnam's Sons, 1914.

    6. Hanslick, Eduard, *The Beautiful in Music,* trans. Gustav Cohen. Indianapolis: The Liberal Arts Press, Inc., 1957.

D. Expressionism

    7. Meyer, Leonard B., *Emotion and Meaning in Music*. Chicago: The University of Chicago Press, 1956, pp. 1–6. The first section of Meyer's book presents the three views and his intentions in exploring them.

    Supplementary readings on Expressionism will be given for the next 5 chapters. For an introduction, see Beardsley (1, pp. 342–55) on "Semiotic Approaches."

CHAPTER
THREE

art and feeling

Throughout history the appeal of art has been recognized to be wider than purely intellectual. The "emotions," the "feelings," the "affections," the "passions," have all been assumed to be a necessary part of art and sometimes are assumed to be the most important part of art. But how, precisely, is art related to feeling? Exactly what role does "emotion" play in art? Answering these questions is hardly an academic exercise: unless the educator has a clear understanding of how art and feeling relate he cannot possibly be efficient in his task of helping other people understand and share the affective nature of art.

The answers given by Referentialism and Formalism are clear even though contradictory. For the Referentialist the emotions of art are the same as the emotions of life. The artist captures his emotion in the art work. The art work transmits the captured emotion to the perceiver. To the extent that an artist's emotion is a noble one, and to the extent that he can infect other people with it through the intermediary of his art work, the artist is good, the art work is good, and the effect on the perceiver is good.

If one were a teacher of art one would select good art works; that is, art works which transmit good emotions; and do everything one could to insure that one's students felt the particular emotion the art work contained. If the teacher is effective in smoothing the way from the artist to the art work to the student, so that a minimum of emotional ambiguity creeps in, the teacher is successful in his job, or at least in this important aspect of his job. What would the teacher actually have to do to be successful? First, he would have to decide which emotion is being presented. Clues could come from the circumstances of the artist's life at the time he created the work, from the title of the work if the artist (or someone else) was considerate enough to attach a helpful title to it, and from the references to emotion contained in the work. If none of these sources prove helpful the teacher must make an "interpretation"—an educated guess, so to speak. He then helps his students go through the same process, by discussing the artist's life and what he may have felt when he made the work, what the title signifies, what the subject matter in the work suggests as to a likely emotion, and, finally, by encouraging interpretations if, as is unfortunately often the case, the emotion proves elusive. Once identifying the emotion in question, or at the very least the *possible* emotion in question, the teacher can then focus the students' attention on the emotion in order to clarify its meaning and value in life.

Absolutism disagrees with all of this, and the Formalist would probably disagree violently. In fact, Formalism was and is primarily a reaction against the excesses of a romanticism which indulges in fanciful, emotionalized interpretations of art works. To counter what they considered an unconscionable overemphasis on art's referential content, Formalists insisted on the purely artistic nature of art, even to the point of denying the possibility of any connection between art and emotion. It is not surprising that excesses on the side of "purity" occurred, to balance out the excesses of referential "impurity." It is also not surprising that when one looks closely enough at the writings of most Formalists, one finds that a recognition of art's connection with feeling does in fact exist, but with feeling as an aesthetic component rather than a non-aesthetic component of art works. (4).

There is no particular problem in understanding the extreme positions about art and emotion; that art deals with emotion non-artistically or that art deals with emotion not at all. And the educational implications of each are clear. One either teaches referentially, as described above, or one dismisses any concern with feelingful reactions to art, concentrating one's teaching on the purely formal components of art works in as intellectually rigorous a fashion as one can devise. But neither position is convincing, aesthetically or educationally. The experiences most people have with art testify to the existence of feeling, but feeling as somehow different from the emotions outside art. And to teach either by separating emotion from the artistic context in which it arises, or by ignoring the existence of feeling, seems to miss the point of art's peculiar emotional appeal. How can the existence of feeling in art be explained without recourse to the extremes of Referentialism or of Formalism, and how can instruction take advantage of the particular kind of feelingfulness art arouses?

A look at several common notions about art and emotion will help us answer these questions. The first and perhaps most widely held is the idea that art—music specifically—is a "language of the emotions." This idea, of course, guides Deryck Cooke's discussion and also Tolstoy's. Every Referentialist view includes a "language-like" conception of how music functions. According to such a view, the essential element of anything which can be called a "language" is present in music. This essential element is a *vocabulary*. A vocabulary is a collection of symbols, each one of which has an agreed upon reference, and which can be combined in various ways to produce more complex references. Words as used in conventional ways are symbols. Numbers, sounds such as the dots and dashes of Morse code, movements or positions such as semaphore code, graphs of various kinds used in scientific reports, picturizations such as hieroglyphics, systems of lines and dots such as musical notation, all these and many more are symbol-systems, or symbolisms, made of vocabularies, constituting "languages."[1]

According to the Referentialist, musical sounds are conventional symbols, in that they have meanings which can be agreed upon and which can be translated into other symbols such as words. The "meaning" of musical sounds, then, can be stated in words. Of course musical sounds can also be translated into notation, but no one, Referentialists included, considers the notation the "meaning" of the sounds. The question is, can musical sounds be considered to have the same kind of meanings which any language has; that is, meanings which can be specified in a dictionary and translated into equivalent symbols? Can Cooke's translations: a minor second designates "spiritless anguish," a major seventh designates "violent longing," etc., be taken as a dictionary, however primitive, which contains the meanings of music?

The answer given by Absolutism; whether of the Formalist or Ex-

---

[1] The relation of conventional symbols and art-symbols (expressive forms), and the existence of conventional symbols in art works, will be treated in more detail in Chapter Five, "Aesthetic Meaning."

pressionist type, is "No." It is precisely in its "untranslatability"—its difference from language—that the unique value of music or any art lies:

> If all meanings could be adequately expressed by words, the arts of painting and music would not exist. There are values and meanings that can be expressed only by immediately visible and audible qualities, and to ask what they mean in the sense of something that can be put into words is to deny their distinctive existence.[2]

Everyone (Formalists, Expressionists, Referentialists) recognizes that conventional symbols do exist in the arts. Bird calls in music, flowers or fruit in painting, political opinions in literature, bodies in sculpture, all are symbols in the conventional sense of having designated references. The Referentialist contends that *everything* in art is of this symbolic nature. The Formalist denies that the existence of symbols has anything whatever to do with the aesthetic "meaning" of an art work. The Expressionist recognizes that a symbol in an art work contributes to the art work's expressiveness, *but only in so far as the symbol becomes immersed in the aesthetic qualities of the work.* To the extent that a symbol remains a symbol in the conventional sense, in which sense a symbol is also a "sign" or a "signal," its meaning is meaning in the usual sense. Such meaning is not aesthetic.

These ideas can now be clarified in regard to "emotion." If a piece of music designates a particular emotion, say "grief," as portrayed in a Baroque melodic formula or in a silent movie piano accompaniment to a particularly heart-rending event, the Referentialist would maintain that "grief" is the emotional meaning of the music. He would also maintain that *all* good music has such emotional designation; that is, that all good music is a language of emotion. A major criterion of "goodness," for the Referentialist, is the music's degree of effectiveness as a symbol or sign of emotion.

The Formalist would say that the melodic "grief" formula, either in the Baroque work or the "pit piano" piece, may indeed by a symbol of grief, but that this symbol contributes nothing to the emotion the work arouses. If the formal properties of the music are excellently constructed and presented the piece will be good, whether or not an emotion-symbol happens to be present.

The Expressionist assumes that so long as the "grief" formula is distinct from the aesthetic qualities of the music which contains it, and is

---

2 John Dewey, *Art as Experience* (New York: Capricorn Books, 1958), p. 74. Reprinted by permission of Capricorn Books.

regarded as a distinct entity—as a bit of "language"—it is not yet aesthetic in expressiveness. If, however, the formula, along with its designation, becomes an integral part of the sounds which are expressive *as sounds,* so that it loses its identity as a symbol while at the same time it contributes to the total effect of the piece, then the formula becomes part of the aesthetic content of the music. As salt adds flavor to a stew, losing its character as grains of salt but adding a particular flavor to the stew, the symbol must be dissolved in the musical sounds, losing its character as a symbol but adding its symbol-flavor to the total piece.

If a piece of music happens to contain an emotion-symbol (most pieces do not), the music is good to the extent that the symbol becomes dissolved in expressive sounds which are *themselves* good.[3] So long as music remains at the level of language it is non-aesthetic. So long as responses to music are responses to emotional designations, the responses are non-aesthetic. So long as teaching gives the impression that emotion-symbols, when they are present, are the emotional meanings of music, or that music devoid of symbols (as most music is) can be translated into emotion words, the teaching is non-aesthetic.

Music, then, is not in any sense a language. It is neither a non-verbal language (such as numbers or musical notation or dots and dashes, etc.), nor an indefinite language nor a tonal language nor a language of the emotions. For music *as music* lacks the essential characteristic of any language; its terms (sounds) can not be defined or translated. Musical sounds are not conventional symbols. As we shall see, this fact is the basis for the enormous power music has to do what language can not do.

Another common idea about the relation of music and emotion is that music is "expression of emotion." According to this idea, the composer uses sounds as a symptom of his emotional condition at the time he is composing. The sounds are a "working off" of his emotions, serving a purpose similar to slamming doors or pounding his pillow or slapping his forehead. To the degree that the composed sounds embody the emotion the composer is feeling, they are successful as music. This idea is an obvious application of the view that music is an emotional language.

To be really effective as an expression of emotion, or as "self-expression," one's behavior must be physical, overt, intimately connected to the emotion one is having at the moment. "Jumping for joy," "wringing one's hands in sorrow," "shaking with fear," "screaming in terror," "sobbing with grief," "beaming with happiness," all are effective expressions of emotion. They constitute, in fact, as exact a "language of

---

[3] Chapter Seven discusses the means by which sounds become musically expressive.

emotions" as we are likely to ever have. Each physical act is a symbol of an emotion, and together they form an emotional "vocabulary." None of them, it must be noted, requires any sort of artistic form. They are spontaneous, un-selfconscious, uncontrolled in form even if moderated by the existence of onlookers. If a person's behavior seems rehearsed, selfconscious, controlled in its form, we suspect very strongly that the expression of emotion is not genuine—that a certain dispassionate element has entered in—that the person is just "going through the motions."

If an artist were really "expressing" the way he felt at the moment of creation, his "work" would hardly be artistic. It would lack the aesthetic qualities, expressive in *themselves*, which must be present if an art work is to be distinguishable from an emotional symptom. The better a particular behavior is as an expression of emotion, the less likely it is to contain aesthetic qualities which are themselves expressive. The creation of expressive aesthetic qualities requires, in addition to intense involvement, a "working out" process which comes from controlled thought, and such thought is foreign to emotional discharge:

> . . . an inner agitation that is discharged at once in a laugh or cry, passes away with its utterance. To discharge is to get rid of, to dismiss; to express is to stay by, to carry forward in development, to work out to completion. A gush of tears may bring relief, a spasm of destruction may give outlet to inward rage. But where there is no administration of objective conditions, no shaping of materials in the interest of embodying the excitement, there is no expression. What is sometimes called an act of self-expression might better be termed one of self-exposure; it discloses character—or lack of character—to others. In itself, it is only a spewing forth.[4]

Whether a creative musician is a composer or a performer, the more his music is "self-expression" the less it can be aesthetically expressive. Consider, for example, jazz, much of which contains as high a level of immediate feelingfulness as any style of music. When the jazz performer's personal involvement is transformed into musical materials which are expressive as music, the effect can be very powerful aesthetically. As soon as musical quality disappears, so that the trumpet's shrieks are shrieks pure and simple, adding nothing to the musical expressiveness of the piece, the performance has become non-aesthetic. It may be moving, or perhaps embarrassing, depending on one's reaction to witnessing another person giving vent to his emotions, but it is not aesthetically expressive. The performer in the concert hall whose "interpretation"

---

4 Dewey, *Art as Experience*, pp. 61, 62.

approaches self-expression is particularly painful to regard, for we do not go to a concert to be onlookers of emotional self-expression; either of a composer or a performer:

> Now, I believe the expression of feeling in a work of art—the function that makes the work an expressive form—is not symptomatic at all. An artist working on a tragedy need not be in personal despair or violent upheaval; nobody, indeed, could work in such a state of mind. His mind would be occupied with the causes of his emotional upset. Self-expression does not require composition and lucidity; a screaming baby gives his feeling far more release than any musician, but we don't go into a concert hall to hear a baby scream; in fact, if that baby is brought in we are likely to go out. We don't want self-expression.[5]

The reservations stated about music as language apply with equal force to music as self-expression: so long as music remains at the level of "expression of emotion" it is non-aesthetic. So long as responses to music are responses to a particular emotion which is assumedly being "expressed," the responses are non-aesthetic. So long as teaching gives the impression that "self-expression" is what is occurring in music, or encourages "expression of emotion" while dealing with music, the teaching is non-aesthetic. These facts are the basis for the unique ability of music to do what "expression of emotion" can not do.

Having dismissed the conceptions of music as a "language" of emotion and as "expression" of emotion, the next logical and necessary step can be taken toward an understanding of music's expressive power; that is, to dismiss the conception of music as dealing with "emotion" at all. This is not in any sense to adopt the Formalist view of music as an intellectual exercise; rather it is to use words very carefully to help us distinguish subtle but important differences between expressiveness which is aesthetic and that which is not.

All of human experience is permeated with subjective responsiveness. Far from being little "computers on legs," humans are creatures whose every act and every thought, from birth to death, is suffused with feeling. Feeling is part of human life as air is part of human bodies; it is as difficult to conceive human life without feeling as without air. And much of what we "know" about our world—of what our world seems to us to be like—we "know" about by feeling about it. Our feelings are not just "added on to" our human existence, as a separate element overlaying

---

5 Reprinted with the permission of Charles Scribner's Sons from *Problems of Art*, p. 25, by Susanne K. Langer. Copyright © 1957 Susanne K. Langer.

our physical or intellectual being; feeling saturates everything we are and do and is inseparable from everything we are and do. The nature of the human condition is very largely a nature of feelingfulness.

Let us call the feelingfulness of human life "subjective reality"— the element in reality of human responsiveness (some other terms are listed in column two on page 25. Human subjective reality is endlessly varied and infinitely complex. Its possibilities are inexhaustible, both in breadth and in depth. And subjective reality is part of all human reality: there is no "real" for humans without the element of the subjective. (Chapter Six will expand on this idea.)

In the vast realm of subjective reality a few guideposts exist, marking off large areas of feeling which are somewhat related to one another or which share a particular, subtle shading. These guideposts, which are little more than occasional buoys in an ocean of subjective responses, have been given names. One of them, for example, is called "love." Love is a category-word, and what it categorizes is an infinite number of possible ways to feel, these ways being somewhat related to one another. The breadth and depth of feeling which falls under the category "love" is so large and complex, so subtle and varied, that the word used as a category for it can only indicate its most general character. Even if one qualifies the word by adding others: parental love, romantic love, puppy love, platonic love, one is only adding a few more buoys to the ocean, each one of which is surrounded by a huge expanse of water. Parental love is another category word for another limitless complex of possible feelings. In fact, trying to "narrow down" feeling by using more descriptive category-words tends to have the opposite effect: each new category calls attention to a whole new realm of possibilities of feeling.

Another factor makes the realm of human subjective reality infinite in complexity and scope. This is the indistinctness of human feeling. Think of the possibilities of feeling categorized by the word "hate." Surely, as the history of humankind shows, these must be infinite. Now think of the possibilities of "fear." Again, an infinite realm of feeling. Are these two categories really separate? Is there not a great deal of "fear" in "hate"? Could we not add a few more category-words to flavor the pot? How about "envy" and "suspicion"? Each word categorizes a huge realm of possibilities of feeling, and each overlaps the others in a welter of intertwined responses. The closer we look at subjective reality the larger and more complex it becomes, and the smaller and more insignificant become the category-words we apply to it.

For purposes of clarity, let us agree to call all the category-words we could possibly think of "emotions." And let us call what takes place in the infinite realm of subjective reality "feeling." Feeling itself is incapable of being named, for every time we produce a name we are only producing a category. So the difference between "emotion" and "feeling" is a real one—it is the difference between words and experiences, the one being only a symbol (or sign) of certain possibilities in the other:

> Save nominally, there is no such thing as *the* emotion of fear, hate, love. The unique, unduplicated character of experienced events and situations impregnates the emotion that is evoked. Were it the function of speech to reproduce that to which it refers, we could never speak of fear, but only of fear-of-this-particular-oncoming-automobile, with all its specifications of time and place, or fear-under-specified-circumstances-of-drawing-a-wrong-conclusion from just-such-and-such-data. A lifetime would be too short to reproduce in words a single emotion.[6]

Human experience is always accompanied by feeling, but our ability to stipulate what is being felt is limited by the extreme limitations of category-words, which are incapable of pinpointing the immense complexity and fluidity of subjective responsiveness:

> We are given to thinking of emotions as things as simple and compact as are the words by which we name them. Joy, sorrow, hope, fear, anger, curiosity, are treated as if each in itself were a sort of entity that enters full-made upon the scene, an entity that may last a long time or a short time, but whose duration, whose growth and career, is irrelevant to its nature. In fact emotions are qualities, when they are significant, of a complex experience that moves and changes . . . Experience is emotional [feelingful] but there are no separate things called emotions in it.[7]

Music can present a sense of human feeling because music is, in Dewey's words, "a complex experience that moves and changes." When attention is paid to the unchanging or constant aspect of music, a particular emotional shading can sometimes be identified which characterizes the piece. This particular identifiable emotional shading is usually called "mood":

> Because music flows through time, listeners and critics have generally been unable to pinpoint the particular musical process which evoked the affective response which they describe. They have been prone, therefore, to characterize a whole pas-

---

6 Dewey, *Art as Experience*, p. 67.
7 Dewey, *Art as Experience*, pp. 41–42.

sage, section, or composition. In such cases the response must have been made to those elements of the musical organization which tend to be constant, e.g., tempo, general range, dynamic level, instrumentation, and texture. What these elements characterize are those aspects of mental life which are also relatively stable and persistent, namely, moods and associations, rather than the changing and developing affective responses [feelings] with which this study is concerned.[8]

There is no doubt but that music can designate moods, just as it can designate other things. But as with all designation in art, the thing designated must enter into the aesthetic components of the work if it is to contribute to the aesthetic effect of the work. So long as mood remains the object of attention, isolated from the aesthetic use of mood in the work as a whole, the response has not yet become aesthetic. If a particular work has such a heavy load of mood-designation that little if anything remains for the expressiveness of the sounds themselves, the work is to that extent non-aesthetic. The difference between "Music to Make You Misty" and Debussy's prelude "The Girl with the Flaxen Hair" is not the particularity of the mood, which is no doubt more obvious in Jackie Gleason's music, but in the amount and quality of musically expressive contents *in addition to* and *including* the mood-designation.

If the only means available to humans to help them understand their nature were language—whether words or some other type of designative system—a major part of human reality would be forever closed off to comprehension. The subjective part of reality—the feelingfulness of human life—cannot be brought into view for perceiving and understanding through the use of language. This is not because no one has taken the time to think up enough words to name all possible ways of feeling; it is because the nature of feeling is ineffable in essence.

Because language cannot be used to help us understand the nature of feeling it would seem at first thought that subjective reality cannot be understood at all; that it must remain in the dim, nether world of the incomprehensible. This is not the case, however. Humans *can* understand more about the nature of feeling; they *can* grow in their comprehension of the breadth and depth of human subjectivity. In so far as it is possible for people to do so, and in so far as people succeed in doing so, the quality of their lives will be affected by the quality of their self-understanding. They will have deepened their insight into a major—perhaps *the* major—aspect of the human condition: subjective responsiveness.

---

[8] Leonard B. Meyer, *Emotion and Meaning in Music* (Chicago: The University of Chicago Press, 1956), p. 7. Other typical statements about the distinction between emotion (or mood) and feeling are: (6, p. 22), (7, p. 8), (3, p. 372).

The arts are the means by which humans can explore and understand subjective reality.

How does art do this? Three components of the art-process must be explained in order to show how art serves its peculiar function of making the subjective comprehensible. These are 1) the creation of an art work, 2) the way an art work presents a sense of feeling, and 3) the experience of an art work. The next three chapters are devoted to these topics. For the present the implications of the view of art as expressive of the life of feeling can be made explicit.

Art works do not tell us about feeling the way psychology does. That is, art works do not "conceptualize about" feeling. Instead, their aesthetic qualities present conditions which can arouse feeling. In the direct apprehension of these aesthetic qualities we receive an "experience of" feeling rather than "information about" feeling. And this "experience of" is the particular, peculiar, unique way that insight into the nature of feeling can be gained. The arts are the most powerful tool available to man for refining and deepening his experiences of feeling:

> Because the forms of human feeling are much more congruent with musical forms than with the forms of language, music can reveal the nature of feelings with a detail and truth that language cannot approach.[9]

Every art "reveals the nature of feelings" in its own, particular way, and the major function of every art work is to do precisely that. It would not be possible to make this assertion if the word "feelings" were interpreted in a narrow sense, as "emotion" or as a shading of emotion called "mood." What is meant by "feeling," to re-emphasize this point, is infinitely broader than "emotion," in that it includes every possible mode of responsiveness of which humans are capable. The many new departures in contemporary art, for example, are not in any sense negating or denying human feelingfulness: they are, instead, opening up whole new dimensions of responsiveness for exploration and understanding. Far from being "anti-human," as so often asserted by its critics, contemporary art is showing, perhaps more dramatically and abundantly than ever before, the staggering potential for responsiveness of which the human organism seems capable. In this sense, new departures in art, *when successful,* expand the possibilities of human self-understanding by presenting new "experiences of" the seemingly limitless realm of subjective reality.

---

9 Susanne K. Langer, *Philosophy in a New Key* (New York: Mentor Books, 1942), p. 191. Reprinted by permission of Harvard University Press.

Every good work of art, no matter when it was made and no matter how it was made, is good because its aesthetic qualities succeed in capturing a sense of human feelingfulness. The depth of feelingfulness presented by art's aesthetic qualities can range from the most superficial to the most profound. Any success at all in capturing and presenting a sense of "expressiveness," that is, of "feelingfulness," is artistic success to that degree. If a particular piece of music is genuinely expressive—if it presents in its aesthetic qualities a sense of feeling—it is a good piece of music. A simple song which is lovely (by which is generally meant that the song is expressive) is a good piece of music. The deeper the sense of feeling captured by a piece of music, the more profound its expressiveness and the more powerful its presentation of insights into subjective reality, the "better" is the work. At some point along the scale of goodness a work can be called "great." Of course no simple number-scale can be applied to the differences in quality between art works, but the combined judgments of sensitive people can serve as a rough guide to the level of goodness of particular works, ranging from good to great. If no sense of feelingfulness is presented by the work, it can be called either "bad" art or "non-art." (This idea will be developed further in Chapter Seven.)

Notice that no stipulation whatsoever is being made about what *kind* of feelingfulness a work should present. Goodness is not a function of kinds of expressiveness, in which there are "good" feelings or "bad" feelings. The entire realm of human experience is open to exploration and understanding through art. People often limit their experiences of art to a particular kind and to a particular level of goodness. But no such limitations can be placed on art itself, which is as limitless as is human responsiveness itself.

The major function of art is to make objective, and therefore conceivable, the subjective realm of human responsiveness. Art does this by capturing and presenting in its aesthetic qualities the patterns and forms of human feelingfulness. The major function of aesthetic education is to make accessible the insights into human feelingfulness contained in the aesthetic qualities of things. Aesthetic education, then, can be regarded as the education of feeling. (5, p. 8).

When music education is regarded as aesthetic education, its major function is the same as that of all aesthetic education. One way of stating this function (others will be suggested in succeeding chapters) is that music education is the education of human feeling, through the development of responsiveness to the aesthetic qualities of sound. The deepest value of music education is the same as the deepest value of all aesthetic education: the enrichment of the quality of people's lives through enriching their insights into the nature of human feeling.

How would one teach music in order to realize its deepest value? That is, how can music education be aesthetic education?

Several principles suggest themselves. First, the music used in music education, at all levels and in all activities, should be good music, which means genuinely expressive music. Because of the belief that only certain *kinds* of expressiveness are good, music education has tended to use music which is generally "polite"; which is safe, bland, sweet, well-behaved, these qualities reflecting the values of most educators. But if music education is to widen children's understanding of the possibilities of human responsiveness, a more open, more free-wheeling, more adventuresome attitude needs to be taken toward "proper" musical materials. Music of the many ethnic and cultural groups in American society, music of the past and much more music of the present, music of various types—jazz, pop, folk, as well as concert—all should be considered "proper" sources for finding expressive music.

Second, opportunities must constantly be provided for the expressive power of music to be felt. This means that the experience of the work as a unified thing must come first and last. If the aesthetic quality of music is the most valuable part of music, and if this is the part which is to be made accessible to children through the efforts of teachers, then music's aesthetic quality should not be obscured by methods which concentrate so exclusively on details that music's total impact is seldom, if ever, experienced.

Third, the most important role of music education as aesthetic education is to help children become progressively more sensitive to the elements of music which contain the conditions which can yield insights into human feeling. These elements—the expressive qualities of melody, harmony, rhythm, tone color, texture, form—are totally objective: they are identifiable, nameable, capable of being manipulated, created, discussed, isolated, reinserted into context. There is nothing mystical about musical events and how they give rise to a sense of significance. While the affective response to aesthetic elements in music is indeed ineffable, the elements which can arouse the response are not. They are the teacher's stock in trade, constituting the basic materials for teaching and learning at every level and in every activity.

Finally, the language used by the teacher should be appropriate for his purpose, which is to illuminate the expressive content of music. An appropriate language is one which is descriptive and never interpretive. Words must be carefully chosen for their power to call attention to the events in music which present the conditions for feeling. But words should never stipulate what that feeling should be. Only one thing can properly cause feelingful responses to music: the sounds of the music themselves. Words which attempt to influence feelingfulness inevitably interpose themselves between the music and the perceiver, preventing the music itself from working its power. No one has a right to place himself between music and people—least of all the music educator.

These principles are the most germinal of the many which can be drawn from the position that music education should be primarily aesthetic education. They will be repeated briefly after the next three chapters, each time viewed in the light of each chapter's particular concern. The final chapters will apply them to the music education program, showing them in operation as guides to aesthetic education in music.

QUESTIONS FOR DISCUSSION

1. Why is it dangerous to think of music as a "language of emotions"? When people use this phrase do they 1) mean it literally and precisely, 2) mean it poetically and suggestively, 3) not usually know just what it means?

2. Can you think of analogies other than "salt flavoring a stew" for the idea that an emotion or a mood can be assimilated into the total aesthetic expressiveness of an art work?

3. What are some other "expressions of emotion" than those given? Why does it not make sense to say that artists are "expressing their emotions" through art?

4. Can you think of analogies other than "buoys (emotions) floating on an ocean (feeling)" to suggest the differences between emotions and feeling?

5. Why is it non-aesthetic or pre-aesthetic to teach about emotion or mood as being what art works are about?

6. What is the difference between the way psychology deals with feeling and the way art deals with feeling?

7. Should there be some limitations put on the kinds of feelings art should deal with or should art be allowed to explore the ocean of feeling freely and fully?

8. Give tangible examples which carry out the principles that in music education 1) genuinely expressive music should be used; 2) opportunities must be provided for the expressive power of music to be felt; 3) focus should be on that in music which contains the conditions of expressiveness; 4) an appropriate language should be used.

SUPPLEMENTARY READINGS

1. Baensch, Otto, "Art and Feeling," in *Reflections On Art*, ed. Susanne K. Langer. New York: Oxford University Press, 1961, pp. 10–36. Probably the clearest statement of the view that art objectifies the subjective.

2. Dewey, John, *Art as Experience*. New York: Capricorn Books, 1958, pp. 58–70. Other sections of Dewey's classical book on aesthetics will be listed after following chapters.

3. Ducasse, Curt J., "The Aesthetic Feelings," in *The Problems of Aesthetics*, ed. Eliseo Vivas and Murray Krieger. New York: Holt, Rinehart & Winston, Inc., 1965, pp. 368–76.

4. Fry, Roger, "Pure and Impure Art," in *A Modern Book of Esthetics*, ed. Melvin Rader. New York: Holt, Rinehart & Winston, Inc., 1962, pp. 304–09. This is an excellent example of the recognition by a supposed Formalist of the feelingful nature of art as defined in the present book.

5. Langer, Susanne K., "The Cultural Importance of the Arts," in *Aesthetic Form and Education*, ed. Michael F. Andrews. Syracuse University Press, 1958, pp. 1–8. An accessible but profound explanation of aesthetic education as the education of feeling.

6. Langer, Susanne K., *Problems of Art*. New York: Charles Scribner's Sons, 1957. Chapter 2, "Expressiveness," pp. 13–26. Other chapters of this useful book will be listed as appropriate.

7. Meyer, Leonard B., *Emotion and Meaning in Music*. Chicago: University of Chicago Press, 1956, pp. 6–22. Meyer further develops, in this section, his view on the relation of art and affect.

CHAPTER
FOUR

aesthetic creation

Much of the world in which humans live can be regarded for its aesthetic qualities, whether or not it was intended for that purpose. All of nature can be regarded aesthetically. Man-made things such as machines, which were made to serve other than aesthetic purposes, can also be regarded aesthetically. A work of art is a man-made thing, and its primary purpose is to be regarded for the aesthetic qualities it contains. The work may serve many other important functions: it may earn a living for the person who made it, it may be part of a social ceremony, it may provide pleasant personal contacts for people engaged in its production, it may be a good financial investment, etc. But the peculiar thing about a work of art—the characteristic which makes it different from things in nature or other man-made things—is that the aesthetic qualities it captures and presents can be regarded as a major reason for its being. When art is regarded as art, rather than as social or political commentary, as an item of trade, as a means to any non-artistic ends, it is as a bearer of aesthetic quality that it exists in the first place.

The interest of this book is in art as art, and in the value of art for people through education. While it is obvious that art also serves non-artistic ends, it is with art's aesthetic function that aesthetic education should be primarily concerned. This point of view leads to the question of how aesthetic qualities are created in a work of art. If the major function of art is to capture and present, in its aesthetic qualities, insights into the nature of human feelingfulness, it is important that those who teach art have a clear idea of how the process of artistic creation works.

Several notions about aesthetic creation have already been implicitly discussed. It was maintained, for example, that art is not "self-expression" or "expression of emotion." This means that the process of aesthetic creation is not a process of releasing emotional energy by making something which is a symptom of how one happens to be feeling at a particular time. The process of creation is not, therefore, a "working off," but is, instead, a "working out." But precisely how does one "work out" aesthetic qualities so that they are captured into something called a work of art?

A helpful way to approach this question is by contrasting the process of communication and the process of aesthetic creation. In the difference between these two processes lies the unique power of aesthetic creation to capture a sense of the patterns of subjectivity—a power not available in the process of communication. Mixtures of the two processes will be discussed after an explanation of how each works as a separate phenomenon.

Several conditions must exist in order to call a process "communication." First, the communicator (say, a person), must select, from all possible messages, a particular message which is to be transmitted. The message may be some information, an opinion, an emotion, a command, etc.

The message is then encoded into a signal[1]—words, dots and dashes, bodily movements, numbers, etc.—which transmit the message to a receiver (say, another person). The receiver then changes the signal, or "decodes" the signal back into the message (the signal "please close the door" is decoded into a message about a desired action). All this may happen instantaneously, as in normal discourse, or it may be a prolonged process, as in the writing of a book. In the latter case, the author selects a particular set of facts, opinions, assertions, etc., and encodes them into words which are transmitted by means of ink and paper. The reader decodes the inkmarks on the paper back into words which give him the author's message.

In order for communication to be successful, a minimum of inter-

---

[1] A signal is what we have previously called a conventional symbol. Discussions of the communication process commonly use the more technical terms "signal" or "sign." All of these words will be discussed in more detail in the next chapter.

ference should be involved between the communicator's message and the receiver's understanding of it. Interference may occur at every step along the way. For example, the communicator could choose a poor signal for his message. Instead of saying "please close the door," which is the message he wants to transmit, he might say "no one ever cares about privacy around here." The receiver may indeed "get the message" that the door should be closed, but a great many other possible decodings could take place instead. Because of the ambiguity involved, we could say that poor communication is taking place.

Another opportunity for interference in the communication process arises in the "decoding" phase. A guest in a foreign country, being left in his hotel room by a bell-hop, may say "please close the door." The bell-hop cannot decode the signal because he does not understand English. He looks puzzled, trying to figure out what message is being transmitted. Again, poor communication is taking place.

If communication is to be *good* communication, the communicator must begin with a clear idea of what is to be transmitted; he must translate the message into signals which exactly represent his message; and the signals must be decoded in just the right way by the receiver. If all these things happen the message will have gotten from the communicator to the receiver intact. Good communication will have taken place.

Nothing about the process just described applies to the process of aesthetic creation.

The first important difference between communication and aesthetic creation is that the artist does not begin with a message. What starts the process of creation is an "impulse," often disembodied, sometimes attached to an artistic idea such as a melody or a combination of words or a set of contrasting colors. Whatever the initial impulse, it is not a formulated message—conceptual or emotional—which then is encoded into a signal. Instead, it is a tentative motion—a sense of possibility—a germinal idea which seems to have the power to grow. The act of aesthetic creation lies precisely in the growth process; and this process is radically and fundamentally different from the process of choosing proper signals to transmit a preexistent message. In fact, to the extent that an artist follows the communication process rather than the creation process his work will turn out to be non-artistic: "music that is invented while the composer's mind is fixed on what is to be expressed is apt not to be music. It is a limited idiom, like an artificial language, only even less successful."[2] Langer

---

2 Susanne K. Langer, *Philosophy in a New Key* (New York: Mentor Books, 1942), p. 195.

The growth process which is the essential characteristic of aesthetic creation is a process of *exploration*. It is a searching out and discovering of expressiveness. The exploration into subjective reality takes place through an exploration of the expressive possibilities of the medium in which the artist is working. There is no way for humans to explore the realm of feeling except through exploring the feelingful qualities of things—words, sounds, colors, shapes, movements, acts. Aesthetic creation explores and forms the feelingful qualities of a particular medium. And this exploring—forming process is in no way, shape, or form a process of encoding messages:

> Creation in the fine arts is, no doubt, not a process in which an idea springs forth in the artist's mind, to be mechanically worked out in some material; it involves feeling out the possibilities inherent in the stone or the pigments.[3]

Two typical statements by composers apply this notion directly to musical creation. Aaron Copland says,

> Every composer begins with a musical idea—a *musical* idea, you understand, not a mental, literary, or extramusical idea . . . The idea itself may come in various forms. It may come as a melody . . . or . . . as a melody with accompaniment . . . or, on the other hand, the theme may take the form of a purely rhythmic idea . . . Now, the composer has the idea. He has a number of them in his book, and he examines them in more or less the way that you, the listener, would examine them if you looked at them. He wants to know what he has . . . Every composer keeps in mind the possible metamorphoses of his succession of notes. First he tries to find its essential nature, and then he tries to find what might be done with it—how that essential nature may momentarily be changed.[4]

Compare this statement by Roger Sessions:

> The process of execution is first of all that of listening inwardly to the music as it shapes itself; of allowing the music to grow; of following both inspiration and conception wherever they may lead. A phrase, a motif, a rhythm, even a chord, may contain within itself, in the composer's imagination, the energy

3 Monroe C. Beardsley, *Aesthetics* (New York: Harcourt, Brace & World, Inc., 1958), p. 33.
4 Aaron Copland, *What to Listen for in Music* (New York: McGraw-Hill Book Company, Inc., 1957), pp. 23–25. With permission of McGraw-Hill Book Company, Inc.

which produces movement. It will lead the composer on, through the force of its own momentum or tension, to other phrases, other motifs, other chords.[5]

In the process of discovery which constitutes the act of aesthetic creation the creator himself is introduced to new possibilities of feeling. His own understanding of subjective reality is expanded and deepened through his work:

> As the painter places pigment upon the canvas, or imagines it *Dewey* placed there, his ideas and feelings are also ordered. As the writer composes in his medium of words what he wants to say, his idea takes on for himself perceptible form . . . the physical process develops imagination, while imagination is conceived in terms of concrete material.[6]

It is clear, then, that the communication process, which consists of choosing unambiguous signals (symbols) to carry a preexistent message, is quite different from the process of aesthetic creation, which consists of an exploration of the expressiveness of a particular medium. If one were to diagram the difference between communication and aesthetic creation, one might do so as follows:

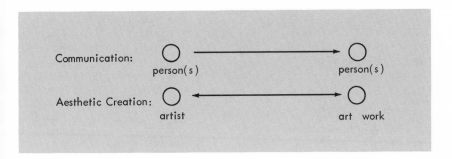

Communication tries to get a message from the sender to the receiver as directly as possible, with as little interference as possible from the thing (the signal) which carries the message. The signal (words, noises, gestures, etc.) is of interest only insofar as it transmits the message. The expressive, or aesthetic qualities of the signal are quite beside the point for communication. In fact, if the transmitting medium is too

---

[5] Roger Sessions, "The Composer and his Message," in *The Creative Process*, ed. Brewster Ghiselin (New York: The New American Library, 1955), pp. 45–49. Copyright Princeton University Press, 1941.

[6] Dewey, *Art as Experience*, p. 75.

interesting in and of itself, it can only get in the way of "good" communication.

The double arrow in the diagram of aesthetic creation indicates the reciprocal effect of the artist and his medium. The artist works on the medium and the medium works on the artist. This interchange is precisely the condition which allows for exploration to take place. In the quality, intensity and profundity of the interchange lie the conditions for the quality, intensity and profundity of the thing created out of it. If the artist's involvement with his medium, as he explores its expressive potentials, is of high quality—sensitive and skillful and imaginative; if his involvement is intense—strong and keen and vivid; and if it is a profound involvement, calling into play the artist's deepest sense of the nature of feeling; the product—the art work—is likely to be of high quality, intense expressiveness, profound insightfulness. The thing created contains its quality and intensity and profundity *because of the interaction* between artist and medium.[7] This is far removed from the communication function of signals chosen to carry a message with a minimum of interference.

Aesthetic creation is different in degree from "making." The difference between "making" something (say, a bookcase) and "creating" a work of art is that in the process of aesthetic creation the involvement with the medium is essentially for the purpose of exploring and capturing its expressive potential. Any non-expressive concerns are quite peripheral. In making a bookcase the essential concern is its functional character while any aesthetic qualities it displays are peripheral. If the bookcase shows a high degree of concern with its appearance as an expressive object, we begin to call it a "creation," acknowledging that its purely aesthetic qualities are an important component. Similarly, if a so-called "non-functional" thing (say, a song) is very weak in aesthetic quality but strong in non-aesthetic concerns, such as the "clean, fresh taste" of the cigarette it extols, we hesitate to call the song a "creation," but are likely to regard it as being as "manufactured" as the product it is serving. If the song were so interesting aesthetically that people forgot the product in their enjoyment of the purely musical qualities of the commercial (a rather unlikely occurrence), the song-writer could justifiably be accused of being "too creative."

Between the two poles of purely aesthetic "creation" and purely utilitarian "making" are many points where things contain both qualities. A well-designed automobile should be a delight for the eye as well as a safe, efficient means of transportation. A well-designed lamp should

---

7 Some comments about art works which contain little if any of this interaction—which are not "created" in the sense being explained here—will be made in Chapter Seven.

provide aesthetic enjoyment in addition to being an efficient source of light. A piece of utilitarian writing—a newspaper editorial, for example—is essentially communication, but can also contain a great deal of aesthetic quality in its artistic use of words.

If we move a little further along the line between pure utility and pure aesthetic quality, we eventually come to a point where we call a thing a work of art, even if at the same time it has a utilitarian function or a communicative function. A novel (say, Hemingway's *The Sun Also Rises*) is a work of art, but it is also, secondarily, a piece of communication. A piece of program music (say, Berlioz' *Symphonie fantastique*), is a work of art, while at the same time it communicates some specific, non-artistic information.

At this point we have explained the essential difference between communication (or "making") and aesthetic creation, and have also shown how the two can overlap. The next chapter will treat the "overlap" in some detail, because it is important that teachers of the arts be clear about the differences and similarities between the aesthetic and the non-aesthetic. For the rest of this chapter our concern will be with the process of aesthetic creation as a distinctive phenomenon, quite different in intent and technique from the process of communication. The point of view of the philosophy being developed is that the primary concern of aesthetic education is *the realm of the aesthetic.* The implications for aesthetic education of the distinctive nature of aesthetic creation must now be drawn.

As an artist "works out" the expressive possibilities of his medium he is at once embodying his understanding about the nature of feeling and exploring new possibilities of feeling. The thing he creates contains his insights into subjectivity, capturing both what he brought as a person to the act of creation and what he discovered during that particular act of creation. The art work, then, can contain the artist's insights as they exist up to and including that particular work.

The perceiver of the work, upon experiencing its expressive qualities (Chapter Six discusses the characteristics of aesthetic experience), both *shares* the artist's insights into subjective reality captured in the work's expressive qualities, and *explores* new possibilities of feeling opened to him by the work's exploratory nature. So the experience of the work is both a sharing and a discovering. In this sense it is also a *creative* experience for the perceiver, in that new insights into feeling are made possible as he grasps more and more of the work's expressive subtleties.

But note that the "sharing" which takes place between the artist and the perceiver is not in any sense an outcome of *communication* between the artist and the perceiver. The sharing takes place through the art work, and the art work is not a signal of a message being transmitted by its creator. If one regards an art work as a bit of code it would be proper to ask the artist what he intends to communicate by means of that code. The artist, of course, did not intend to "communicate" at all, or he would not have made an art work. Instead, he would have chosen some proper signal to clearly and unambiguously transmit his message. If regarded solely as communication, a complex work of art can only be judged a complete flop. It lacks everything good communication ought to have. This is why many people become very annoyed with an art work when they cannot figure out what "message" it might be transmitting. They are likely to ask, about a complex poem, for example, "Why doesn't the poet just come right out and say what he means?" The fact that the poet might have labored long and hard to get the poem to be just what it turned out to be, and that it would have been a simple matter for the poet to state a message if that was his intention, escapes anyone who goes to a work of art expecting to find "communication."

What takes place between the artist and the perceiver, then, is not communication but "sharing." The sharing occurs by means of the art work, which contains an embodiment of insight about feeling, this embodiment capable of giving rise to insights into feeling on the part of the perceiver. The perceiver's insights can not be precisely those of the creator. In the first place, the creator has not made a simple statement of a message but a complex set of aesthetic qualities capable of giving rise to many and varied insights. In the second place, the creator is one person and the perceiver is another. Each will respond differently to the aesthetic qualities created or perceived in the work, by virtue of their different lives. At the same time, each will share a sense of significant insight into human feeling, by virtue of their sharing of the common human condition.[8]

It is precisely in this sharing of insight into the common nature of humanity that art exercises its humanistic effects. There is no more powerful way for humans to explore, embody and share their sense of the significance of human life than through the making and experiencing of art. When the act of creation has taken the artist deep into the nature of human existence; when the perceiver similarly but individually shares the sense of the human condition embodied in the art work; both creator and perceiver have been carried below the surface differences and divisions of daily life to a point where the common humanity of people can be glimpsed and felt:

---

[8] Compare Dewey, *Art as Experience*, p. 54.

The secret of artistic creation and the effectiveness of art is to be found in a return to the state of *participation mystique*—to that level of experience at which it is man who lives, and not the individual, and at which the weal or woe of the single human being does not count, but only human existence. This is why every great work of art is objective and impersonal, but none the less profoundly moves us each and all.[9]

Jung

The power of art to cut through the surface of life and to give a sense of life's depths makes art man's most effective tool for deepening the insights of people into their shared nature. "In the end, works of art are the only media of complete and unhindered communication [sharing] between man and man that can occur in a world full of gulfs and walls that limit community of experience."[10] This sharing is, in essence, humanistic, for it allows people to know—through actual experiencing rather than through preachments—about the common estate of men.

If education is to be humanistic in its effects it can be so more effectively through art than through any other means. In order for art education to be humanistic it must be primarily *aesthetic* education. That is, education in the arts must help people share the insights contained in the aesthetic qualities of art works, for that is where the insights into human subjectivity lie. The insights are available in the work of art itself, and the function of aesthetic education is to make those insights available by showing people where and how to find them. One does not find them by asking their creator what he was trying to communicate. One finds them *by going deeper into the aesthetic qualities of the created work.* A diagram of this process adds a second dimension to the diagram of aesthetic creation presented earlier:

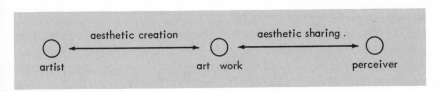

aesthetic creation   aesthetic sharing .

artist   art   work   perceiver

In aesthetic sharing (or aesthetic experience) the perceiver actively involves himself in the aesthetic qualities of the art work, "For to per-

---

[9] Carl G. Jung, *Modern Man in Search of a Soul* (New York: Harcourt, Brace, & World, Inc., 1933), p. 195.

[10] Dewey, *Art as Experience,* p. 105.

Dewey

ceive, a beholder must _create_ his own experience."[11] The art work, at the same time, works its power on the perceiver, shaping his experience by the shape of its expressive content.

The process diagrammed here is called "communication" by many writers about art, because of the existence of what we have chosen to call "sharing." These writers (John Dewey and Leonard B. Meyer, among others) are very well aware of the distinction between actual communication and aesthetic creation, of course, but choose to continue to use the word "communication" as descriptive of the particular kind of sharing which takes place in the art process. The reader must exercise his own judgment about the gains and losses in using a word with a commonly accepted meaning to describe a process which is not at all like what the word is commonly taken to mean. Because of the importance of the distinction between actual communication and aesthetic creation for techniques of teaching art, the word communication will be avoided in this book. It is also suggested that teachers of art avoid the word "communication" in their teaching, because of the inevitable confusion it arouses. Students of every age have some notion of what communication is or should be, and very naturally expect art to comply when art is described as communication. It is no wonder, therefore, that so many people seek in art for what is not there—communicated messages —and are confused and disappointed when they do not find them. Aesthetic educators can help dispel this confusion, and help people look for what _is_ in art, by judicious use of words which, at the very least, do not confuse the issue. Langer's statement in this regard about music is equally applicable to all the arts and should be taken seriously by all

Langer

teachers of the arts: "Not communication but insight is the gift of music; in very naive phrase, a knowledge of 'how feelings go.' "[12]

Where, precisely, can one find the insights in art works so that they may be shared? Every mode of art has its own characteristic elements for creating expressive forms. The aesthetic or expressive elements of music are rhythm, melody, harmony, tone color (including dynamics), texture and form. A similar list can be made for every art. In painting, for example, characteristic aesthetic elements are color, line, texture, mass, etc. In poetry are metaphor, imagery, rhyme, meter, structure, etc. In dance are motion, tension and relaxation of muscles, shapes, design, weight, etc. Every order of art has a well developed domain of expressive materials for exploring and understanding subjective reality.

The present chapter has dealt with aesthetic creation in its usual

---

11 Dewey, *Art as Experience*, p. 54.
12 Langer, *Philosophy in a New Key*, p. 198.

sense of composing, painting, sculpturing, writing. The performing arts —music, dance, theater—include another aspect of aesthetic creation in that the original act of creation must be given tangible form by a "re-creator"—the performer. The creativity of performance will be discussed in Chapter Nine, in the context of the values of the performance program. Creativity of still another sort is present in aesthetic experience, as briefly mentioned in this chapter. Some further comments will be made about this aspect of aesthetic creation in Chapter Six.

The major function of aesthetic education, it has been suggested, is to promote the fullest possible sharing of the insights into human subjectivity contained in the aesthetic qualities of things. In light of the discussion of aesthetic creation, this suggestion takes on an added dimension. Aesthetic education should help people share as fully as possible in the created aesthetic qualities of art works, so that their insights into feeling can be both shaped by the artist's own insights and broadened by being given the opportunity to explore new insights.

How can music education fulfill the major function of aesthetic education?

First, the music used in music education, at all levels and in all aspects of the program, should be music which contains, in its created aesthetic qualities, conditions which can give insights into human feeling. Not every bit of music used in teaching will plumb the depths of the human psyche, nor be a masterpiece of aesthetic excellence. The criteria for selection of music are 1) genuine expressiveness, 2) the possibility of at least some of the expressiveness being shared by the particular students being taught, 3) the impetus for discovering new shades of feeling through discovering new aesthetic qualities in the piece, and 4) the addition of some further ability to share the insights in a wider variety and complexity of music.

Second, opportunities must constantly be provided for the created aesthetic qualities of a work to be shared. The total impact of the music must come first and last, with systematic exploration of its subtleties in between. The teaching process should never get in the way of aesthetic sharing, but should illuminate aesthetic qualities of the music in a context of aesthetic experiencing of the music.

Third, teaching which effectively increases the ability of children to share and explore the sense of feeling in musical works must focus on that in the music which *contains* the conditions of feeling. Aesthetic education in music—or any art—is no seance-like waiting for mystical spirits to appear. It is an active searching out of the conditions—objective conditions—through which insights into feeling can be shared and explored.

Finally, the techniques and the language used by the teacher to focus attention on the aesthetic qualities of music should never interpose themselves between the students and the music. If a technique distracts attention from the aesthetic qualities of the sounds in a particular piece, that technique is a hindrance to aesthetic education. An example of this is the technique of having children draw pictures "illustrating" a piece being listened to. Aside from falsely assuming that the aesthetic qualities of one medium can be translated into another, this technique insures that attention to the sound itself will be at a very gross level. It does nothing to call attention to the subtle qualities of sound which are most affective, but instead redirects attention to something quite extrinsic to the music itself.

It is also possible for language to get in the way of fuller musical sharing. Teachers who in their zeal try to get their students to feel what the teacher thinks they *should* feel, by the use of emotion-words which influence feeling, can only undermine the unique value of aesthetic creation and aesthetic sharing, which must be allowed to be as truly personal as anything in human life can be. The availability of helpful language makes the use of obstructive language quite unnecessary.

Two more dimensions will be added to these principles, as the next two chapters raise issues about two more dimensions of aesthetic education in music. The more broadly conceived the principles become, the richer will be their implications for the music education program.

QUESTIONS FOR DISCUSSION

1. Give some examples of the communication process as it works 1) when it is fully effective and 2) with some obstacles to effectiveness.

2. Discuss the differences between encoding a message, as in communication, and searching out qualities of expressiveness, as in aesthetic creation. What are the implications of these differences for what one should expect to find in an aesthetic creation?

3. How does the process of creation change the creator? What does this suggest about the strong urge of artists to continually create new works?

4. Give some examples of utilitarian things which have such a high degree of aesthetic quality that one might very well call them "art works." Give some examples of non-utilarian things which are so lacking in aesthetic quality that you would hesitate to call them "art works."

5. Why is the word "sharing" more suggestive of what takes place between the artist and the perceiver than the word "communicating"?

6. Why is the word "humanising" descriptive of the outcome of aesthetic sharing?

7. Give tangible examples of 1) where in music one goes to find created aesthetic qualities, 2) how one would help others find these qualities and share their expressiveness.

SUPPLEMENTARY READINGS

1. Copland, Aaron, *What to Listen for in Music.* New York: McGraw-Hill Book Company, Inc., rev. ed., 1957, Chapter 3, "The Creative Process in Music." Although written for non-musicians, some helpful insights into various aspects of the musical process are given in this book.

2. Dewey, John, *Art as Experience.* New York: Capricorn Books, 1958, pp. 70–81. While practically everything in the book is relevant, these pages are particularly so for the topic "aesthetic creation."

3. Kneller, George F., *The Art and Science of Creativity.* New York: Holt, Rinehart & Winston, Inc., 1965. A useful summary of writings on general creativity.

4. Langer, Susanne K., *Problems of Art.* New York: Charles Scribner's Sons, 1957, Chapter 10, "Poetic Creation." Rich implications for all the arts are present in Langer's treatment of poetry.

5. Sessions, Roger, "The Composer and his Message," in *The Creative Process,* ed. Brewster Ghiselin. New York: The New American Library, 1955, pp. 45–49. In addition to Sessions' short selection, this book contains 40 others by artists on artistic creation.

6. Sessions, Roger, *The Musical Experience of Composer, Performer, Listener.* New York: Atheneum, 1962. Chapter III deals with "The Composer," but the entire book is helpful for clarifying aesthetic creation in music.

7. Tomas, Vincent, ed., *Creativity in the Arts.* Englewood Cliffs, New Jersey: Prentice-Hall, Inc., 1964. Various essays on aesthetic creation, the most useful being the last, by Tomas, entitled "Creativity in Art."

CHAPTER FIVE

aesthetic meaning

The problem of aesthetic meaning is a central one in aesthetics and in aesthetic education, because it is difficult to make statements about the arts or the teaching of the arts without implying some notion about what art "means." Many statements about aesthetic meaning have already been made in this book and will be made to its conclusion. The present chapter will attempt to systematize this important topic and show its relevance for aesthetic education. The two chapters preceding this one raised issues which can now be looked at in more organized fashion. The two succeeding chapters will be based largely on the understandings developed in the present chapter. The "centrality" of aesthetic meaning, at least in this book, is literal as well as figurative.

Education consists in large part of the development of people's power to share meanings about man and his world. Aesthetic education contributes to this process through its focus on the particular kind of meaning available in the aesthetic domain. Several kinds or "realms" of meaning exist for humans, each one adding to the totality of the meaning of human experience. A most helpful categorization of the major realms of meaning is given by Philip H. Phenix (7), who identifies six fundamental patterns of meaning which emerge from distinctive modes of human understanding. He calls these 1) symbolics (languages and language-like systems); 2) empirics (sciences dealing in empirical truths); 3) esthetics (primarily the arts, which present unique objectifications of the subjective); 4) synnoetics ("direct awareness" or "personal or relational knowledge"); 5) ethics (moral meaning expressing obligation); and 6) synoptics (comprehensive, integrative meanings as in history, religion, philosophy). (7, pp. 6–7).

While certain aspects of each realm impinge on the others, each can be dealt with according to its characteristic qualities. The concern of aesthetic education is primarily with aesthetic meaning. It is essential that educators in the arts have a good notion of what aesthetic meaning is like, because they constantly deal with this kind of meaning whether they are aware of doing so or not. To the degree an art educator is clear about the kind of meaning present in his subject he can be effective in sharing the meaning and value of his subject with students. This is perhaps too obvious a statement to have to make, but the general lack of understanding about or concern with the meaning of the arts among teachers of the arts makes it necessary in this case to say what should not have to be said.

The views of Referentialists and Formalists on aesthetic meaning are clear and contradictory, as they are on most aspects of the arts. For the Referentialist art acts as communication, transmitting messages containing the same kind of meanings as those which exist outside of art. It is perfectly proper, according to Referentialism, to ask what a work of art means and to expect an answer which stipulates more or less exactly what the meaning is. For those works of art which do not transmit obvious meanings—which contain no representational subject matter or "program"—one must "interpret" the meaning. The primary way to enjoy art, to understand art, to benefit from art, to teach art, is to focus attention on the non-aesthetic meanings which art communicates, either by decoding if this is possible or by interpreting.

The Formalist insists that the meaning of art is totally artistic, having no relation whatsoever to any kind of meaning outside the boundaries of particular art works. Art means itself, which is to say that each work of art is a self-contained system with its own, separate, distinctive meanings. If one is sensitive to the formal relationships in a particular work one can perceive its significance or "significant form." This significance is a function of mutually relevant artistic events, meaningful only within the context of the work.

Expressionists would agree that art *can* communicate non-artistic meanings and that art *can* present mutually related events which are meaningful within the context of art. There is an element of truth in both Referentialism and Formalism, but neither explains the experience of meaningfulness which most people seem to have when creating or responding to art works. This experience contains two elements, which, because of their interrelation, seem to be of a different dimension from either ordinary meaning or exclusively artistic meaning. They are 1) that the sense of meaning in art comes from the *aesthetic qualities* of art, whether or not these include some non-aesthetic meanings, and 2) that the aesthetic meaning perceived in art is meaningful for human life, even as it retains its peculiarly aesthetic quality.

How can a work of art be meaningful *as art* and at the same time be meaningful for human experience? A key idea will help us unlock the answer to this question. This is the distinction between a "conventional symbol" (or "sign" or "signal" or "genuine symbol") and an "art-symbol" (or "expressive form"). (4, p. 127). An explanation of the differences between conventional symbols and art-symbols will help produce an understanding of the peculiar status of art works as meaningful for human life through their meaningful aesthetic qualities.

In the following discussion the single word "symbol" will always mean "conventional symbol." A work of art will be referred to as either an "art-symbol" or an "expressive form." The word "form" in "expressive form" means the total expressiveness of an art work. In music, an "expressive form" is a piece of music, the sum total of its expressiveness being presented by melody, rhythm, harmony, tone color, texture, form (in the narrower sense of structural organization) and whatever else contributes to its musical affectiveness. All of this together is an "expressive form" or "art-symbol."

Four elements are necessary in order to produce both a symbol and an expressive form.[1] These are 1) the subject—the person who will make the symbol or the expressive form, 2) the object—the thing about which the symbol or expressive form will be made, 3) the symbol or expressive form itself, 4) the conception which the symbol or expressive form gives about the object—the conception given by 3) of 2).

Suppose that you are 1) the subject, and that you are going to make a conventional symbol. The symbol will be of 2) an object, which in this case will be the paper, ink, glue, etc. at which you are now looking. The symbol 3) you will make will be a sound. The sound will begin with a soft explosion made by your lips, continue with a flapping of your vocal

---

[1] These elements are based on the discussion in Charles Leonhard and Robert W. House, *Foundations and Principles of Music Education* (New York: McGraw-Hill Book Company, Inc., 1959), pp. 84–85.

cords, and end with a harder explosion made by the back of your tongue and your soft palate. The sound-symbol is as follows: "book." (Aren't you clever?) Your symbol gives 4) a conception which is quite specific. A "book" is a particular thing with particular properties. We can look up your symbol ("book") in the dictionary to find out what the commonly accepted "meaning" of it is. If you wanted to be more specific in your calling up of a conception through a symbol, you could make your symbol a bit more complex— "paperback book," or "philosophy book," etc. If you wanted to be very specific about this particular book you could make a five-page series of symbols—a "book report." However simple or complex, the process, including elements 1)–4), will be similar. It should be clear that the symbol-making process is a restatement of the communication process explained in Chapter Four, and the language process mentioned in Chapter Three.

Symbols can give conceptions of ideas as well as things. The word "beauty" is difficult to define because so many, complex elements are involved in the idea of beauty. Nevertheless the word can be called a symbol, in that it does satisfy the four elements of symbol-making, including element 4); a conception about which it is possible to agree.

The same is true about many other things commonly called symbols. A dove is called a symbol of peace. A skeleton is a symbol of death. A halo is a symbol of holiness. A serpent symbolizes evil. All these words are conventional symbols (or "signs" or "signals" or "genuine" symbols) because they give an agreed-upon conception. The terms "art-symbol" and "expressive form" are being reserved, therefore, for the unique kind of thing which is a work of art. We are reserving the terms "art-symbol" and "expressive form" for art works because of the very distinctive difference between an art work and anything which can be called a conventional symbol.

Let us go through the same four-step process again, this time for an expressive form (art-symbol). The subject will be a composer. The "object" with which he deals is "subjective reality," or "human feelingfulness," as discussed in Chapter Three. The expressive form he creates is a piece of music, through a process discussed in Chapter Four. The conception of subjective reality given through his expressive form is quite unlike the conception given by a conventional symbol, in that there is no way to specify, as through a dictionary, the "meaning" of the expressive form. *Yet a conception of subjective reality is given by the expressive form,* and this conception can, in a certain sense, be called "meaning." It is the purpose of this chapter to explain what that "certain sense" of meaning is.

The following diagram shows how our explanation will proceed:

CONVENTIONAL SYMBOLS: SIGNS: SIGNALS: GENUINE SYMBOLS	ART-SYMBOLS: EXPRESSIVE FORMS
non-art	art
information	insight
designative	embodied
consummated; closed	unconsummated; open
general; abstract	particular; concrete
communication	expressiveness
intermediate	immediate
making	creating
discursive form	presentational form
meaning as knowledge	meaning as import

With few exceptions (some religious and personal experiences) meaning outside the realm of art comes from the use of conventional symbols. Science, of course, is the prime example of symbol-meaning, in that the most careful, most controlled use of symbols occurs in this field, yielding very basic knowledge about the world and how it seems to work. The incredible power of carefully used symbols to explain, to predict, to manipulate, to show relations, is the basis of scientific activity and the basis of man's knowledge about the empirical world.

But science is not the only realm of knowing which depends on conventional symbols. Philosophy, history, social studies, languages—all are symbol-using, symbol-knowing fields. The kind of knowledge about ourselves and our world which comes from these "humanities" is symbol-knowledge, dependent primarily on the use of words as a means of discourse. This use of words is a symbol-use, no matter how complex it becomes. So while the non-science realms of symbol-knowing deal with issues different from those which occupy the primary attention of science, both are alike in that the use of conventional symbols is the basic mode of producing meaning.

The arts are unique in that the sense of meaningfulness they produce comes from their nature as expressive forms rather than as conventional symbols. The nature of an expressive form is such that a single, agreed-upon meaning acceptable to everyone is neither possible nor desirable. This is quite the opposite of symbol-meaning, which *depends* on agreement as to the meaning of each symbol. One basic difference between conventional symbols and expressive forms, then, is the necessity for full agreement about meaning in the former and the impossibility of full agreement about meaning in the latter. This must not be taken to mean that conventional symbols are precise and expressive forms (art-symbols) are imprecise, however. Each is precise in its own realm but very imprecise when shifted to the other. Expressive forms, as compared with conventional symbols, are quite powerless to give precise knowledge about the factual world. Conventional symbols of any sort—words, numbers, tables, graphs, etc.—are quite powerless to give us precise "knowledge" about human subjective reality, as compared with art, which can do so more "precisely" and with more "truth" than any other means available to man.

The product of symbol-using is information. The information may be about the physical world, about attitudes, about beliefs, about psychological, social, political phenomena. In any case the information given through symbols is primarily of a factual nature. Symbols yield data, simple or staggeringly complex. To all of it the word information is applicable.

The product of art-symbol meaning is insight. Of course the word "insight" is often used to indicate an understanding of deeper levels of the physical or social world. It is used here to call attention to a different dimension of understanding than that available through conventional symbols. This is the dimension of immediate apprehension of the quality of feeling, as presented in the aesthetic quality of something. This kind of discernment yields a "sense of" rather than "information about." The sense of the nature of subjectivity given by an art-symbol is not available through conventional symbols. The expressive quality of the art-symbol itself is what presents the conditions for feelingful response, the product of the response being "insight" rather than factual data.

Conventional symbols point to things other than themselves; they "designate" (or de-*sign*-ate). Because they can do so, symbols allow us to "handle" the objective world to a level of precision equal to the precision of the symbols themselves. This can be a very high level indeed. If it were not for symbols of all sorts we would have no way to refer to ourselves and our world, to share knowledge about them.

But some areas of human experience, by their very nature, are not susceptible of being "pointed to." The only way to explore and understand the realm of subjective responsiveness is to "embody" its shapes and patterns in the shapes and patterns of things. When perceived and responded to, the shapes and patterns of particular things give insights into the same components of subjectivity. Something which embodies a sense of the qualities of feeling in its own shapes and forms is called a work of art or an art-symbol or an expressive form. The "meanings" available from an art-symbol are never pointed to outside of itself, but are functions of the expressive qualities embodied within it.

When a conventional symbol (sign) fulfills its function it gives a specific conception of that which it symbolizes (signifies). The circle from subject to object to symbol to conception is a "closed" one, each element leading around to the next. Such a "closed" symbol is sometimes called a "consummated" symbol. It is consummated because it refers to an agreed upon conception. All symbols, as the word is being used here, are "closed" or "consummated."

Art-symbols do not give a single, agreed upon conception of that which they embody. Therefore the circle from subject (artist) to object (subjective reality) to art-symbol (expressive form) to conception (insight into the patterns of subjectivity) remains "open" or "unconsummated." The conception given by the art-symbol is a creative, personal, subjective sharing—a "sense of" meaningfulness rather than a stipulated bit of data. All art-symbols (expressive forms), as the word is being used in this book, are "open" or "unconsummated." This does not mean that *no* conception is given by them, for if no conception is given, the art work is a complete failure (some are). The conception is "open" in that it is not symbolized (designated), but instead is embodied for personal, creative experiencing.

Because of the "openness" of art-symbols and the "closedness" of conventional symbols one might think that art deals in the general and abstract and science deals in the specific and concrete. But the opposite is true. The information given by science about the world is used in the service of generalizations and abstractions about the world:

> To know a science is to be able to formulate valid general descriptions of matters of fact . . . . Science is characterized by descriptions which are essentially *abstract*. It does not deal with the actual world in the fullness of its qualitative meanings. Rather, certain carefully defined aspects of the experienced world are selected as the basis for scientific descriptions. Different sciences deal with different aspects of the experienced world, using different schemes of abstraction.[2]

---

[2] Philip H. Phenix, *Realms of Meaning* (New York: McGraw-Hill Book Company, 1964), pp. 95–96.

Science is one of the most effective means available to people to learn about the general nature of things. This is because of its ability to move from data to abstractions about the data:

> . . . in logic, mathematics, or science . . . the customary way to pass from concrete experience to conceptions of abstract, systematic relation patterns is through a process of generalization—letting the concrete, directly known thing stand for all things of its kind. Even when scientific thought has not reached the abstract level—when it still deals with quite concrete things, like apples or cubes of wood—it is always general . . . . Wider and wider generalization is the method of scientific abstraction.[3]

How can the qualities of things and events be experienced in their concrete, particular, uniqueness? How can one grasp the meaningfulness of things as they exist as separate entities? Science, philosophy, history, do not offer this kind of "meaning." It is available in the realm of the aesthetic:

> Such, however, is the newness of scientific statement and its present prestige (due ultimately to its directive efficacy) that scientific statement is often thought to possess more than a signboard function and to disclose or be "expressive" of the inner nature of things. If it did, it would come into competition with art, and we should have to take sides and decide which of the two promulgates the more genuine revelation.[4]

The expressiveness of an art-symbol is contained in its aesthetic qualities rather than being pointed to in something outside itself. Conventional symbols have no intrinsic meaning but refer to meanings extrinsic to themselves. Symbol meanings can be communicated (by means of symbols) but art-symbol meanings are available only through an immediate apprehension of quality, and such apprehension is essentially a private adventure.

Conventional symbols are intermediaries for meaning—they are "go-betweens" which show one where to find the meaning they refer to. Art works can give meaning only if we become immersed in their own, singular qualities, with no intermediary between the qualities and the perceiver of them. In this sense the experience of art is "immediate"—

---

3 Reprinted with the permission of Charles Scribner's Sons from *Problems of Art*, pages 32, 33, by Susanne K. Langer. Copyright © 1957 Susanne K. Langer.
4 Dewey, *Art as Experience*, p. 85.

that is, directly felt with no intermediate thing or step between the apprehended work and its expressiveness:

> We never pass beyond the work of art, the vision, to something separately thinkable, the logical form, and from this to the meaning it conveys, a feeling that has this same form. The dynamic form of feeling is seen *in* the picture, not through it mediately; the feeling itself seems to be in the picture.[5]

The telescoping of form and import into a single, immediate experience is a peculiar characteristic of art-symbols. A system of conventional symbols—a language—operates in another peculiar way. All languages consist of "strung-out" symbols; one symbol follows another in single file, accumulating meanings as they go along. This characteristic of language—its "single-file" form—is called "discursiveness." Everything speakable or thinkable by means of language must be spoken or thought of in this linear, discursive form, symbol after symbol after symbol.

According to some people, anything which can not be stated discursively can not be known. Nothing is accessible to the human mind, according to this view, except that which can be put into discursive form; that is, into symbol-languages (sign-languages). (6, pp. 66–69). Everything else in human experience is sheer emotionalism, incapable of being handled objectively or of being known in any real sense.

If this point of view were true, the immediate, expressive, concrete, unconsummated, embodied insights given by created art-symbols could not be described as "knowledge." But human experience has a dimension of meaning beyond that or different from the meaning available through discursiveness. Art-symbols also give meanings, but they do so by gathering up their constituent parts and presenting them for immediate apprehension and response. In an art-symbol the meaning does not come from discrete, intermediary, communicative, abstract, consummated, designative bits of information, as in conventional symbols. The "all-at-once" quality of art-symbols is called "presentational" form, to distinguish it from "discursive" form. (Art-symbols existing in time, such as music, drama, dance, literature, are presentational rather than discursive, even though the "all-at-onceness" is spread out from beginning to end of the art-symbol.) (6, pp. 76–79).

Presentational forms—expressive forms—are the natural mode of articulating subjective reality, bringing this reality into the realm of knowing. Humans *can* know more about their affective nature and therefore about their humanness. But they can not do so through the use of

---

[5] Langer, *Problems of Art*, p. 34.

conventional symbols, which are powerless to capture and present the qualities of things. Expressive forms have this power. Upon being aesthetically experienced, expressive forms yield insights into the qualities of feeling, and such insights are "meaningful" in a way that information can not be.

Because the words "meaning" and "knowledge" have such a strong flavor of "information," some people prefer to use different words to describe the kind of insight given by expressive forms. One such word is "import," which perhaps gives more of a sense of the "insightful" character of aesthetic sharing than do the words "meaning" or "knowledge." (5, pp. 31, 32). Many people insist that "meaning" must be recognized to be far wider than the narrow confines of symbol-system communication, so that the word should be perfectly usable to describe what one receives from art-symbols. Whatever position one cares to take on this matter it is clear that meaning is not confined to conventional symbols. Expressive forms yield meaning also, opening a major realm of human experience to deeper knowing.

It is now possible, in light of this explanation of conventional symbols and expressive forms, to make a pivotal assertion about art and the teaching of art: pivotal because it is a culmination of the book to this point and will serve as a basic notion in the treatment of the topics following it. The assertion is that *in all cases,* works of art should be approached as expressive forms, perceived as expressive forms, responded to as expressive forms, judged as expressive forms, taught as expressive forms. This means that an art work should be approached for insight rather than information, perceived for the qualities which give insight rather than information, responded to as a bearer of insight rather than information, judged on the basis of whether it offers insight rather than whether it offers information, taught in order to share the insights it presents rather than any information it contains. The assertion means that an art work should be approached for embodied meaning rather than designative meaning, perceived as a matrix of embodied meaning rather than designative meaning, responded to for its embodied meaning rather than its designative meaning, judged on how well presented and how deep are its embodied meanings rather than designative meanings, taught in order to share its embodied meanings rather than designative meanings. For every other attribute of an expressive form listed on p. 60, an identical statement can be made, applying the categories of "approaching," "perceiving," "responding," "judging" and "teaching." The effect of this process should be to make crystal clear the very great, very important, very tangible differences which exist between treating art aesthetically (as expressive form) and non-aesthetically (as conventional symbol). Aesthetic education, if it is to be aesthetic in its effects and in its value, must treat art aesthetically.

Must every work of art be devoid of conventional symbols? Certainly not. The line from conventional symbols to expressive forms in the diagram on p. 60 is intended to indicate a continuum. At the ends are things which are entirely conventional symbols or entirely expressive forms, but every point in between contains things which have attributes of both. Many art works, which were conceived as expressive forms and which should in every way be treated as expressive forms, contain some symbol content as part of their expressive qualities. Any symbol in a work of art—any representational subject matter in any of the arts—acts as a conventional symbol, giving information, designating, communicating, etc. So long as a symbol remains a separate element, unrelated to the total aesthetic quality of the art work (which never happens in a successful work of art) it can be regarded separately for its own designation. But every art work which is at all successful incorporates symbol content into its total expressiveness, so that the symbol enters into the work as another element along with, as in music, the expressiveness of melody, harmony, rhythm, etc. In Chapter Three the analogy was given of salt (symbol) flavoring a stew (expressive form) as it enters into the total taste of the stew. Lucius Garvin states the same idea this way:

> Most poems . . . have subject matter. But such subject or meaning, when treated aesthetically, is not, in strictness, the meaning of the poem in the sense that it is something external to the poem that the poem symbolizes. It is the very stuff of the poem; not the whole stuff, but a part which enters into and fuses with the phrases and words and their assonances and rhythms to constitute the poem as an aesthetic organism.[6]

Many statements similar to Garvin's will be found in the Supplementary Readings listed at the end of this chapter. Their implications for understanding art and for teaching art are summarized in a single sentence by Langer: "Representational works, if they are good art, are so for the same reason as non-representational ones."[7] That is, *whether or not* an art work contains conventional symbols, it must be approached, perceived, responded to, judged, and taught as an expressive form. So long as an art work is approached for any of its attributes as a symbol it is being approached non-aesthetically. So long as it is perceived for its

---

[6] "The Paradox of Aesthetic Meaning," in *Reflections On Art*, ed. Susanne K. Langer (New York: Oxford University Press, 1961), p. 64.

[7] Langer, *Problems of Art*, p. 125.

symbol attributes it is being perceived non-aesthetically. So long as it is responded to for any symbol attributes it is being responded to non-aesthetically. Any judgments made about its symbol attributes are non-aesthetic judgments. And, inevitably, when teaching focuses on a work's symbolic content, as separate from the work as an expressive form, the teaching is not yet aesthetic. This is not to suggest that teaching will *ignore* the symbolic content of art works, for to do so would be to ignore an important element in many works of art. It is to point out, however, that so long as attention is being paid to the symbol *as symbol*, teaching has not yet become aesthetic teaching. When the use of the symbol as contributing to the total expressive effect of the work is attended to (when, for example, the "program" element is regarded as an inseparable part of the music's melody, harmony, rhythm, tone color, form), teaching is indeed aesthetic.

The same principle applies when teaching about things falling at the symbol end of the continuum. Many conventional symbols contain aesthetically expressive qualities, even though they are not dominantly expressive forms and therefore are generally not regarded as works of art. It is often useful in aesthetic education to call attention to the aesthetic qualities of things which are not art works, and when this is done the education can legitimately be called "aesthetic." It is so because, as with art works, attention is being paid to meanings which are expressive in quality rather than symbolic. All such teaching is part of the domain of aesthetic education.

The concept of expressive form can be used to distinguish things which are art works from things which are not. A statement which stipulates such a distinction can be regarded as a "definition" of art. But because definitions in the aesthetic realm raise such severe philosophical-linguistic problems it is much more reasonable to regard what look like definitions of art not as final, inclusive, conclusive laws, but much more modestly, as "seriously made recommendations to attend in certain ways to certain features of art."[8] It is as such a recommendation that one may regard the "definition" offered by Susanne K. Langer: art is . . . "the practice of creating perceptible forms expressive of human feeling."[9]

Two aspects of Langer's recommendation have been treated in previous chapters; "creation" in Chapter Four and "human feeling" in Chapter Three. The present chapter has dealt with the "expressive

---

8 Morris Weitz, "The Role of Theory in Aesthetics," *The Journal of Aesthetics and Art Criticism*, XV, No. 1 (1956), p. 35.
9 "The Cultural Importance of the Arts," in Michael F. Andrews, ed., *Aesthetic Form and Education* (Syracuse University Press, 1958), p. 2.

form" part of the recommendation. Taken together, Langer's suggestion is that things which are created aesthetically, which are basically expressive forms rather than conventional symbols (whether or not they contain conventional symbols as part of their expressiveness), and which give a conception of human feeling, can be regarded as "art." Some things are clearly art and some things are clearly not, but there will always be things falling somewhere in between about which judgments must be made. Some people will tend to be conservative about such things, insisting that the "letter of the law" be followed if a thing is to be graced with the word "art." Other people will be quite liberal, calling "art" whatever has even a touch of any of the qualities of art works.

It should be obvious that hard and fast rules simply do not exist in this area. But both history and current events should teach us that people's capacity to invent new modes of exploring, embodying and sharing aesthetic meanings is seemingly endless. It would be easy and safe for aesthetic educators to stick to well established art works, but doing so deprives students of the aesthetic exploration which is, after all, one of the exciting qualities of being involved with art. A "safe" attitude also brands the teacher as a reactionary, looking backward wistfully and forward fearfully. And it removes the opportunity for critical aesthetic judgments to be made about "problem" works. So, while teachers of the arts should not be without guidelines for judgment-making, they should be leaders, openers of doors, seekers of aesthetic adventure among the new, while at the same time helping to make available the proven values of the old.

The primary function of aesthetic education, in light of the concern of this chapter, is to help people share the aesthetic meanings which come from expressive forms. How can music education be aesthetic education? That is, how can music education help people share the aesthetic meanings available in musical expressive forms?

First, music which is genuinely expressive in its characteristics must constitute the core of material for studying and experiencing. Since aesthetic import is not symbol-like it can not be designated, so it is impossible, because of the very nature of art, to choose works according to their "meanings." Instead, one chooses art works because of their aesthetic quality, knowing that the higher this quality the more satisfying, the richer, the more powerful can be the aesthetic meanings shared.

It often happens that an art work's symbolic content is so obtrusive in and of itself that, at least for some people, it prevents the work from being responded to as an expressive form. Examples would be a sensuous nude painting or sculpture used in a junior high school art class or a heavily sacred Christian play used in a Jewish neighborhood or a novel condescending to Negroes used in an inner city high school (or *any* high school), or art songs with very romantic words used in the upper elementary grades, etc. It is true that in each of these cases the work of art should be approached, perceived, responded to, judged and taught as an expressive form rather than as a symbol; that is, for its aesthetic characteristics rather than its non-aesthetic designations. But that is easily said. Good sense would suggest that care be taken before placing such severe obstacles in the way of aesthetic education. One can not simply ignore the world in which people live as one goes about helping them become more sensitive to the aesthetic qualities of the world. A bit of sensible strategy would seem in order, to avoid fruitless barriers to aesthetic learning while at the same time helping to make more and more of the aesthetic components of the world accessible to all children.

Second, the experience of music as expressive form is the be-all and end-all of music education, for such experience is the only way of sharing music's aesthetic meaning. This indicates that musical experience itself should come first and last. The "pay-off" of music education—the sharing of music's aesthetic meanings—should be central, with all means focused toward that end and actually producing that end at every possible moment as learning proceeds.

Third, the study of music—the means for reaching aesthetic ends—should concentrate on those characteristics of sounds which make them expressive. The embodied, expressive, unconsummated, presentational character of sound is objective in every sense. It can be systematically taught for, both as a component of all music and as the specific aesthetic content of particular pieces. The skillful teacher will help students get closer and closer to the sounds of music, so that the sounds themselves— the tone-conditions of melody, harmony, rhythm, tone color, texture, form, which embody musical insights—can exert their affective power.

Fourth, the language and the techniques used by the music educator must be true to the nature of music as expressive form. It would be a great mistake—perhaps a fatal mistake—for teachers to assume that because the meaning of an expressive form can not be verbalized, words are therefore not useful for teaching aesthetically. Language remains a basic means toward aesthetic ends. The best language for this purpose, paradoxically, is the most symbol-like language, giving useful information, designating precisely the important components of musical events, making helpful generalizations about how music works, communicating specific data about the conditions of sound which can yield aesthetic meaning.

The role of the music educator as aesthetic educator—which is to make accessible the aesthetic meanings of music—is an active, directive, involved one, calling for a high degree of musical sensitivity and pedagogical expertise. To help people share aesthetic meaning is no simple task, but it is perfectly capable of being fulfilled by good teachers. In this, aesthetic education is no different from any other kind of education.

QUESTIONS FOR DISCUSSION

1. How would you teach for aesthetic meaning if you were 1) a Referentialist, 2) a Formalist? Give specific examples for other arts as well as for music.
2. What might be some implications for teaching several subjects together of the fact that philosophy, history, social studies, are "symbol-knowing" fields while the arts yield import from expressive forms? Are there some inherent contradictions in teaching both "humanities" and "arts" together?
3. If the nature of an art-symbol is such that its "meaning" cannot be stated in language (in conventional symbols), what is one to make of the many available "interpretations" of the meaning of art works? Do such interpretations foreclose possibilities for aesthetic import to be shared?
4. How do you feel about the words "meaning" and "knowledge" as applied to the insights available from art? Do you think it is permissible to use these words or would you rather limit them to the product of conventional symbols? What educational advantages and disadvantages accrue from 1) using these words, or 2) avoiding their use in teaching art?
5. Try to apply the operations of "approaching," "perceiving," "responding," "judging," and "teaching" to each of the listed attributes of an art-symbol. Can you give examples of educational practices suggested by the various combinations? Do some persuasive, underlying practices suggest themselves?
6. In light of the important differences between conventional symbols and art-symbols, why is it suggested that a very powerful tool for teaching aesthetically is precise, unambiguous words, which are, after all, the prime example of conventional symbols?
7. What difficulties are raised for teaching the arts in general and music in particular, by the element of conventional symbol meaning contained in various works of art? How can such meanings obstruct aesthetic meanings from being shared? How can they be used in the service of sharing aesthetic meanings more fully?

SUPPLEMENTARY READINGS

1. Dewey, John, *Art as Experience*. New York: Capricorn Books, 1958. The chapter, "The Expressive Object," treats aesthetic meaning in a most interesting, incisive way.

2. Garvin, Lucius, "The Paradox of Aesthetic Meaning," in *Reflections On Art*, ed. Susanne K. Langer. New York: Oxford University Press, 1961, pp. 62–70. A short but extremely useful discussion.

   Because the topic of aesthetic meaning is a crucial one in Susanne K. Langer's thought, she has written abundantly on its various aspects. The following are among her most important writings on this subject:

3. Langer, Susanne K., *Mind: An Essay on Human Feeling*. Baltimore: The Johns Hopkins Press, 1967, Chapter 3, "Prescientific Knowledge." In this volume, the first of a three-volume work now in progress, Mrs. Langer's views on human feeling reach a high point of articulation. Chapter 3 is a storehouse of ideas about aesthetic meaning.

4. Langer, Susanne K., *Problems of Art*. New York: Charles Scribner's Sons, 1957. Chapter 3, "Creation." Among the important ideas in this chapter is that of the "sensory illusion," a key to understanding Langer's concept of aesthetic meaning. See also Chapter 9, "The Art Symbol and the Symbol in Art." In informal language Mrs. Langer discusses art as expressive form and the existence of conventional symbols in art.

5. Langer, Susanne K., *Feeling and Form*. New York: Charles Scribner's Sons, 1953. Chapter 3, "The Symbol of Feeling." This keystone book in Langer's edifice of thought contains her most detailed explanations of each major order of art. Chapter 3 lays some groundwork for all the arts as she understands them.

6. Langer, Susanne K., *Philosophy in a New Key*. New York: Mentor Books, 1942. Chapter 4, "Discursive and Presentational Forms," makes very clear the incapacity of discursive languages to conceptualize all that humans can know.

7. Phenix, Philip H., *Realms of Meaning*. New York: McGraw-Hill Book Company, 1964. Although the chapter on Music (pp. 141–151) is too elementary to be of use, its first four pages give a fine overview of some of the unique qualities of aesthetic meaning.

8. Sontag, Susan, *Against Interpretation*. New York: Farrar, Straus & Giroux, Inc., 1961. A widely discussed and immensely interesting book, in which Mrs. Sontag, in the first chapter, explains the irrelevance of "interpreting" works of art. (Her famous essay "Notes on 'Camp' " is contained in this volume.)

CHAPTER SIX

aesthetic experience

Aesthetic education aims toward the fullest possible sharing of the expressive power in the aesthetic qualities of things. Much has been said in the previous chapters about aesthetic sharing, but this aspect of aesthetic education is so important that separate attention must be paid to it. Exactly how does one get from art what art can give? And how does one help *others* get from art as much as they are capable of getting? No questions are more important than these for people who are responsible for teaching the arts.

For the Absolute Formalist aesthetic sharing is different in kind from any other sharing in human life. To discuss the way people relate to the aesthetic qualities of things is to discuss an isolated area of human responsiveness, having its own special character and its own special value.

The Referentialist, at the other extreme, takes the position that aesthetic sharing is no different from many other kinds of sharing. Communication is communication, no matter what symbol-system happens to be in use. So one should not treat the idea of aesthetic responsiveness differently from any other kind of responsiveness, nor expect that any value different in kind rather than degree can come from aesthetic sharing as compared with other types.

The position to be taken here, consistent with those the Absolute Expressionist takes about other major aspects of aesthetics, is that aesthetic sharing is indeed a particular kind of sharing, having characteristics which give it an identifiable quality of its own. At the same time aesthetic sharing permits a major component of human life to be more fully known—to be more fully "shared." The connection between aesthetic sharing and the realm of human feeling is so close and so profound that it is probably impossible to discuss one without implying the other. It will be helpful at this point to begin with a closer look at the realm of feeling than was taken in Chapter Three, working our way back to a concept of aesthetic sharing from a better understanding of human feeling.

Every living thing exhibits the same basic condition: an interaction between the thing and its environment. This interaction is a constant process of accommodation; of impulses received and given; of movement and counter-movement. The characteristic quality of life is a pervasive state of flux in which the organism moves from imbalance to balance, from tension to relaxation, from agitation to stasis, from need to fulfillment, from action to rest. As long as an organism continues to respond to its surroundings it is alive. When interaction stops life has stopped.

Human life is permeated with the movement—the rhythm—of organic existence. At the cellular level myriad changes take place in a constant movement from growth to decay. Muscles and organs play their part in the ongoing flux of living. At the preconscious level hundreds of occurrences exhibit the fact that the organism lives: eyes blink, lungs fill and empty, sensations are received and responded to. At the lower levels of consciousness countless small acts exhibit the rhythm of existence: we sit, stand, reach, grasp, chew, stretch, walk, bend, look, hear. As we organize the sensations of life into conscious constructs the scope of life's rhythm gets larger. We sit down to a meal, eat, and finish. A class starts, the hour progresses, the class ends. An evening begins, several people meet, go out, come home. Morning comes, the day starts, many things happen during its course, night comes, the day is over. Monday morning rolls around (inevitably), we go through the week, the weekend comes, another week has passed. The curve of life's rhythm becomes broader as larger sections of life are lived: the passing of the seasons, the passing of the years, the time of childhood, of youth, of middle age, of old age. The totality of a life is itself an overarching curve of movement, containing beneath it an infinite number of smaller and smaller rhythms. And all earthly life together can be conceived as the broad arch of livingness, under which all separate lives play out their separate but common rhythms.

Because of the intimate connection between movement (taken in the broad sense of "ongoingness" or "interaction") and life itself, anything which exhibits a rhythmic motility seems to be touched with significance. We watch the waves moving in from the sea or lake, gathering energy, dashing on the shore, retreating with energy spent. The fascination of this sight goes much deeper than its sheer sensuous pleasure. We get a sense, wordless but strong, of import—of "the way things are." Similarly for many other rhythmic phenomena: the gathering storm, its energy, its dissolution; the fading of day, the sunset, the coming of darkness; the first signs of spring, the budding of trees and flowers, the greenness of summer. All give a sense of the essential quality of livingness.

Two characteristics of human beings lead from the conditions of livingness to aesthetic experience. First, humans are capable of perceiving movement as a bearer of significance. This kind of perception is quite different, for example, from seeing an egg in the sand along a barren seashore and knowing that life exists in a seemingly lifeless place. The egg is a symbol of life, the word "symbol" being used in light of all the information given about it in the previous chapter. The significance of movement, on the other hand, is not a symbol of life, but an embodiment of the conditions of livingness. As in every such embodiment, the significance, or import, or insight, or expressiveness, is inseparable from the very shape and form of the thing which embodies the movement. The expressive form does not "point to" life, as does the seabird's egg, but presents embodied conditions which are immediately (without an intermediary) grasped as significant. The ability to respond to the significance of expressive forms is a basic, pervasive, peculiar characteristic of human beings.

The second human characteristic which leads to aesthetic experience is an extension of the first. Humans are not only capable of responding to things as aesthetically expressive, they are capable of transforming their sense of the significance of movement into expressive forms. Human beings create and respond to expressive forms not as an adjunct to their lives—as a pleasant activity for spare moments—but as an essential component of their nature.

Art works are expressive forms in which the conditions of livingness have been captured so that people can regard them and understand them. The conditions of life—the rhythms of organic existence—are embodied in the aesthetic qualities of art works. In music, for example, the aesthetic qualities presented by melody, harmony, rhythm, tone color, texture, form, are expressive of or analogous to or isomorphic with the patterns of felt life or subjective reality or the conditions of livingness. (Other terms for this notion are given in the list on page 25.) When we perceive the conditions of livingness embodied in the aesthetic qualities of a thing, and react to the expressiveness—the feelingfulness—of those aesthetic qualities, we can share the sense of "aliveness" presented by those aesthetic qualities. To the extent that the expressiveness of a work is deep and vital, and to the extent we can share that expressiveness by perceiving and reacting to the conditions which contain it, our sharing of a sense of organic life will be deep and vital. This sharing of insights into the nature of life, through perceiving and reacting to aesthetic qualities which are expressive of the nature of life, is called "aesthetic experience."

The position being taken here as to the biological or "natural" basis for aesthetic experience is very strongly based on the thought of John Dewey (2) and Susanne K. Langer, among a great many others. Langer especially has built her system of aesthetic thought on a "naturalistic" base, the most profound statement of her position (and perhaps the most important treatment of the biological basis of the arts in the entire literature of aesthetics) being *Mind: An Essay on Human Feeling*.[1] The reader wishing to expand his understanding of the relationship between art and life should spend some time with Langer's book. The point of calling attention to it here is to establish the position that art is not esoteric or rarified or removed from life, but is a basic means for *making contact with life*. The particular way one makes such contact through art is by aesthetically experiencing it.

Although human experience in general is a complex, shifting mixture of countless elements and influences, several characteristics which are peculiar to aesthetic experience can be identified. Whether these characteristics can exist in a "pure state," entirely separated from other elements of experience, is an interesting but academic question. It seems clear that unless these elements are present to some degree the experience would not be described as "aesthetic," and that a clearer notion of what these elements are can help differentiate aesthetic experience from non-aesthetic experience.

One important characteristic of aesthetic experience is "intrinsicality." (5).[2] This indicates that the value of the experience comes from its own, intrinsic, self-sufficient nature. Aesthetic experience is not a means toward non-aesthetic experience and serves no utilitarian purpose. It is experience for the sake of the experience in and of itself, unlike practical experience, the value of which is that it procures something other than itself.

---

1 (Baltimore: The Johns Hopkins Press, 1967.)

2 Several of the terms used here are more fully treated in Schoen's chapter.

In order for an experience to be "intrinsic" it must be removed from pressing, instrumental concerns, so that it can be enjoyed for itself. In this sense aesthetic experience is "disinterested"—not lacking in interest, but lacking in concern about pragmatic outcomes. Another term for this is "psychical distance," which indicates that the person must be sufficiently removed from practical involvement with the experience to be able to lose himself in its own, immediate power.

But while aesthetic experience is intrinsic, disinterested, distanced, it is also involved, outgoing, responsive. Aesthetic experience is much more than detached recognizing or identifying. One's interest and reactions must be absorbed by or immersed in the aesthetic qualities being attended to, calling forth a feelingful reaction (please remember the enormous scope of "feelingful") to the perceived aesthetic conditions. A common term for this involvement is "empathy," which means an identification with or a self-projection into the qualities of the thing to which one is responding. Another phrase indicating the same idea is "tension in repose," the tension being the involvement or empathy, the repose being the distancing or practical disinterestedness.

Aesthetic experience is involvement with expressive qualities rather than with symbolic designations. The involvement is in the embodied qualities of a thing, which have absorbed any designative material which might be present. The experience of the aesthetic qualities is immediate; that is, direct. The particular, concrete, expressive nature of the presented form is what is responded to, rather than any generalized, communicated information the thing may contain. One's whole attitude in aesthetic experience, encompassing all particulars within it, is to regard a thing as an expressive form rather than a symbol, to expect to get what one gets from an expressive form rather than a symbol, to be interested in the thing as an expressive form rather than a symbol. This "aesthetic attitude" is consciously cultivated by the elaborate social behaviors surrounding museums, concert halls, theaters, helping to put people into a frame of mind which encourages aesthetic experience to take place. But the perfectly natural, informal, everpresent need for aesthetic experience makes it a very common, very "every day" kind of occurrence in addition to its occasional formalization into institutional molds.

Finally, aesthetic experience always comes from involvement in the qualities of some perceptible "thing." There is always a sensuous element in aesthetic experience—a presentation to the actual senses. The "thing" may be sounds, words, colors, movements, shapes, spaces, acts; but there must be a thing—"formed substance"—which contains aesthetic qualities to be perceived and responded to.

Let us see how these conditions work out in practice as a guide for distinguishing aesthetic experience from other kinds. Suppose, for a moment, that four men have happened to park their cars at the same time on a "lookout point" by the side of a mountain road. One man is a geologist from a nearby university. A second is a farmer who owns land in the valley below. A third is a clergyman. The fourth man is a music educator (no doubt on his way to a convention). All are looking at the scene below, but each one perceives something different from the others and reacts according to what he perceives.

The geologist thinks, "What an interesting example of glacial movement. The shape of that end of the valley and the way the river runs through it seem to confirm the Schmidt-Eisenson theory of valley formation. I wonder if I should bring my graduate seminar up here to see it." The geologist's experience is "scientific" in the sense that knowledge (information) is its major component. The scene is perceived to be a bearer of scientific information and the reaction is appropriate to that perception.

The farmer looks at his fields below and starts to worry. "Just as I feared," he thinks. "Dry as a chip. I'll have to double the irrigation pipes and this will put me into the red. Maybe I had better go into chicken farming." His perception is of particular signs of growth or the lack of it, and his very practical reaction is a function of what he has perceived.

The clergyman finds himself awed by the grandeur of the scene. "God's works are magnificent," he thinks, and begins to recite a prayer of thanksgiving. Perceiving the valley as an instance of Divine creation, the clergyman's reaction is to offer thanks in an act of worship.

The music educator (aesthetic to the core) perceives the interplay of colors, of shapes, of the texture of the clear sky against the roughness of forest and sparkle of water, of the mass of mountains against the horizon, framing the entire valley. The perceived aesthetic qualities of the scene are enjoyed for their intrinsic loveliness. The scene is felt to be beautiful—to give a sense of pleasure, of significance, of immediately present import. "How lovely," he thinks. And in wordless absorption he "loses himself" in the qualities presented to his vision. His experience is aesthetic.

These four experiences were described as "pure." While they certainly can be so, they also are likely to be mixtures of components of each and of many others. The four men might actually be one man, perceiving differently from moment to moment and reacting differently according to what is perceived. Nevertheless, real differences do exist. The present task is to understand the features of aesthetic experience which are peculiar to it, so that these features can be cultivated through aesthetic education.

Let us suppose now that four people, counterparts of those on the mountain, are standing in front of a painting in a museum. An art historian might regard the painting as belonging to a particular style-period, and try to decide whether it is an "early" or "late" example. An art dealer could perceive the painting as just what one of his wealthy clients is looking for. "How can I get the museum to sell it to me?" he wonders. A religious devout might regard the painting—say, a crucifixion scene—as a religious statement, his experience focusing on the representation in the painting as an event with profound religious meanings. Our ubiquitous music educator perceives the representation as part of a complex set of aesthetic qualities. The entire painting—colors, shapes, lines, masses, textures, bodies—are perceived as intrinsically expressive through their dynamic interrelations.

Again, these four experiences—scholarly, practical, religious, aesthetic—are in actuality likely to be far less "pure" than described. And they are not without influence on each other. Each kind inevitably impinges on the qualities of the others and alters them in some way. And again, our present concern is to differentiate the particular qualities of experience which make it aesthetic, so that we can influence these qualities in appropriate ways.

A final example. Our four subjects find themselves seated together at a concert. The scholar, a musicologist, perceives that the full orchestra is being used to play an early Mozart symphony. "How inappropriate," he thinks. "This conductor certainly doesn't care much about authenticity." Next to him sits the conductor of an orchestra from a nearby city. "If I could pay this Concertmaster enough, I'm sure he'd come to my orchestra," he thinks. "Then I could schedule that violin concerto I've been wanting to do." At his side sits a Nun. "This movement sounds like a part of the Requiem," she says to herself. "The Lord's power is in everything." Finally we come to our music educator (who has had a very busy day). He perceives those qualities which make sound aesthetic—the melody, the rhythm, the harmony, the tone color, the texture, the form—and their fusion into a work which is expressive by virtue of its aesthetic qualities. His reaction is to the perceived aesthetic expressiveness of the music. Through immersion in those conditions of sound which can produce feeling, he responds by sharing the sense of feeling contained in those sounds. His experience of the music, unlike that of his fellow listeners, is aesthetic.[3]

The characteristics which make experience aesthetic can be present

---

[3] The following chapter will discuss musical aesthetic experience in some detail.

in relatively pure form, as with our hypothetical music educator, but they can also exist to some degree in experiences which are not dominantly aesthetic. Some people would take the position that unless the experience satisfies all the conditions of aesthetic experience it should not be called by that name. They would argue that it is possible for an experience to have aesthetic quality without being, properly speaking, an aesthetic experience. A Volkswagen, by way of analogy, has some of the qualities of a Mercedes Benz, but is not a Mercedes Benz. An apple has some of the qualities of a potato, but is not a potato. A hand has some of the qualities of a foot, but is not a foot. A mathematician working at his desk may be intrinsically interested in the developing ideas he is manipulating. He may be absorbed in their interrelations quite apart from any practical use they may have. He may feel that the qualities of his ideas are "beautiful" because of their balance, their progression, their interlocking implications. Can his experience be called "aesthetic?"

Some people would prefer to say that, while his experience has aesthetic quality, it lacks a necessary component of aesthetic experience— a "formed substance" which contains aesthetic qualities regarded as intrinsically expressive. Ideas in and of themselves do not qualify as "things" presented to sense.

Others would be perfectly willing to call "aesthetic experience" any experience which has even the smallest amount of aesthetic quality. This debate is similar to the one about what can be called a "work of art" (page 68). There is no pressing need for a solution to this argument because the obligation of aesthetic education remains the same no matter what position one takes about how purely aesthetic an experience should be in order for it to qualify as "aesthetic experience." The obligation of aesthetic education is to systematically develop the ability of people to perceive the aesthetic qualities of things and to react to the expressiveness of those qualities. To the degree that people can perceive aesthetically and react aesthetically they can share the insights or "meanings" presented by the aesthetic components of things. Some aesthetic perception and some aesthetic reaction must be present in order for any aesthetic experience at all to take place. The task of aesthetic education is to influence that "some"—to make it "more" as a result of teaching and learning.

Aesthetic perception and aesthetic reaction, then, are the two necessary behaviors involved in any experience which is likely to be called aesthetic. The perception and the reaction are simultaneous and interdependent. The perception is not a separate process which later produces reaction, but is inherently "reactive" in nature. What is perceived is perceived *as expressive,* the response being an integral part of the perception. The reaction or response does not take place in isolation. It is dependent on perception of qualities or conditions which can produce reaction in the first place.

It is possible to have a high level of perception with no reaction: this does not qualify as aesthetic experience. Music students taking dictation in theory class are exercising musical perception but are not reacting to the expressiveness of the musical qualities perceived. Few people would call this experience "aesthetic." (The students are reacting, no doubt, but usually with quiet desperation, and this hardly fosters the "disinterestedness" of aesthetic experience.)

It is possible to have a high level of reaction with a bare minimum of perception: this only minimally qualifies as aesthetic experience. The person who goes into ecstasies about a piece of music, who rhapsodizes about the gloriousness of it all—the thrilling, ravishing, blissful delight of the experience, and who at the same time reveals by his remarks that he hasn't the vaguest notion of what went on in the music, can be said, perhaps, to have had an aesthetic experience of a sort, but we need not attach much aesthetic value to it.

The very close interaction which exists between perception and reaction in aesthetic experience exhibits the same qualities as the interaction between perception and reaction in aesthetic creation. It will be remembered from the discussion in Chapter Four that aesthetic creation was described as a process of exploration—a searching out and discovering of expressiveness through the manipulation of some medium. The creator works on the medium and the medium works on the creator. This process was represented as follows:

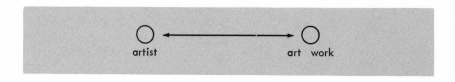

In aesthetic experience we find the same kind of interaction, except that the "searching out and discovering" part does not lead to the creation of a thing. Nevertheless there *is* a searching out and discovering, and this is what has been called "aesthetic perception." Aesthetic perception is an active, outgoing "doing," which intensely involves the person in the aesthetic qualities of the thing being regarded. The aesthetic quality of the thing, in turn, "works on" the perceiver as he becomes aesthetically involved with it, as it does on the creator as he is shaping it. The "doing" becomes an "undergoing," as reaction takes place to what is perceived. The doing—undergoing process, then, is common to both aesthetic creation and aesthetic experience. (2, pp. 53–5). In aesthetic experience the process can be represented as follows:

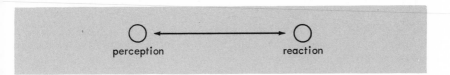

perception   reaction

In the sense of searching out (doing) and reacting (undergoing) an aesthetic experience is a creative experience. It actively involves a person in the creation of new insights through searching them out in the qualities of something in which they are embodied. To expect that the substance of aesthetic experience will be identical for all people who happen to be regarding a particular thing—say, a symphony—is to misunderstand the essentially creative, "personal" aspect of aesthetic experience. Certainly there will be a sharing of insight, because all people share in the common human condition (compare p. 50). At the same time the individuality of every person will insure that his experience has a private dimension. It is this unique combination of the personal and the super-personal which is one of the most satisfying, most fulfilling characteristics of aesthetic experience, in that it promotes a sense of individuality and of commonality at one and the same time. This combination reaches to the roots of the human condition.

Aesthetic perception, as the term is being used here, is a complex behavior composed of many sub-behaviors. When a person "perceives" the aesthetic qualities of a thing he combines behaviors of recognizing, recalling, relating, identifying, differentiating, matching, subsuming, comparing, discriminating, synthesizing, and a host of others both nameable and unnameable. All the components of aesthetic perception are totally objective in nature. They can be influenced by completely objective means. They can be manipulated, discussed, practiced, tested. In short, they can be *taught.*

Aesthetic reaction, on the other hand, is a totally subjective phenomenon. The feelingful content of aesthetic perception can not be named except in the grossest of terms, which, as we have seen, (pp. 36–37) is worse than useless for describing its actual nature. Aesthetic reaction can not be directly manipulated, it can not be isolated for inspection or for practice, it can not be objectively tested. In short, one can not teach directly for aesthetic reaction. To attempt to do so, by discussing people's emotions (feelings, by definition, can not be discussed), by trying to inculcate particular emotions, by suggesting emotion-producing ideas, by any other device which attempts to bypass the necessary and intimate relation of aesthetic feeling with aesthetic qualities perceived, is to violate the nature of aesthetic experience. Nothing more effectively cancels out or distorts the creative, personal, subjective response which is the most valuable characteristic of aesthetic experience than to try to influence that response separately. Only one thing can properly influence aesthetic reaction. That is the aesthetic qualities of things themselves. To the extent that a person can perceive aesthetic qualities keenly, subtly, precisely, sophisticatedly, sensitively, his reaction can be keen, subtle, precise, sophisticated, sensitive.

The major task of aesthetic education, in light of this discussion, is to influence the ability of people to have aesthetic experiences. The ability to have aesthetic experiences can be heightened by education if education concentrates on teaching what is teachable—aesthetic perception—in contexts which encourage creative reactions to that which is being perceived. It is quite possible (and not uncommon) for aesthetic perception to be taught in ways which prevent aesthetic reaction rather than promote aesthetic reaction. This practice is hostile to aesthetic experience because it makes perception a cold, sterile thing and gives the impression that it should be so. To keep in fruitful balance the aesthetic behaviors which can be taught and those which can not, to encourage feelingful responses without doing so non-aesthetically, to guide perception directly enough to make advances while not so intensively that it becomes separated from expressiveness, are teaching tasks as delicate and as difficult as any in the field of education. But while aesthetic educators have a particularly challenging job to do, the rewards of success are concomitantly great, both for the teacher, who is dealing with one of the most fulfilling aspects of human life, and for students, who are gaining more and more of that fulfillment.

The ability to have aesthetic experiences; that is, the ability to perceive aesthetically and react aesthetically, can be called "aesthetic sensitivity." Far from being a mysterious, disembodied phenomenon, aesthetic sensitivity consists of behaviors which are quite identifiable and quite amenable to being developed. The notion that aesthetic experiences and the ability to have them are like exotic flowers, blooming very rarely and only under elaborate hot-house conditions, is unfortunate and untrue, reflecting an "aestheticism" too often cultivated by artists, writers about art, and teachers of art. Aesthetic experience is a hardy weed, growing abundantly and sturdily wherever humans exist. Given conditions friendly to its growth aesthetic sensitivity will flourish, spread, and bear joyful fruits. Under conditions of ugliness (which means conditions devoid of aesthetic qualities), of lack of concern about the quality of people's experience of life, of low expectations for significance as a normal component of experience, aesthetic sensitivity can become stunted and weak.

Whatever the conditions under which it operates, aesthetic education must provide more fertile ground for the growth of people's aesthetic sensibilities than would have existed if there were no aesthetic education. Certainly this is easier under conditions already positive toward the aesthetic in experience. But to think that aesthetic experience is for the privileged, that the pleasures and satisfactions of the aesthetic realm are limited to and proper for particular people only, is to misconstrue the nature of aesthetic sensitivity and the nature of human potential. Aesthetic sensitivity exists to some degree in all human beings, can provide the same delights for all human beings, is capable of development for all human beings. The task of aesthetic education is to deepen the aesthetic sensitivity of all human beings.

A strange notion exists among some people about age as a factor in the ability to have aesthetic experiences. Childhood and youth, according to this view, are periods of preparation for the coming of some glorious future time when one will be "able" to have aesthetic experiences. A proper education, then, consists of preparation. "You may not understand why I'm having you learn this material; you may not find it of any immediate relevance, but take it from me—when you are 'ready' you will be glad I made you learn it." This position, which is not at all rare, is based on a view of children as non-human beings in training to be human beings. Nothing prevents the growth of humanness so effectively as this view. Especially is this the case in the aesthetic realm. Unlike some experiences in life, which, according to law or custom, a person must be at least 21 to legally or morally have, aesthetic experience is normal for children and necessary for children. The first-grader delightedly singing "Twinkle, twinkle, little star," perceiving its lovely contour of melody, its rightness of harmony, its "ongoingness" of rhythm, its balance of form, and "feeling" the expressiveness of the song as musically artful, is having the same *kind* of experience—aesthetic experience—as the crustiest old musicologist absorbed in the complexities of Beethoven's Ninth. The only difference is in *degree*. The job of aesthetic education is to influence that degree.

It should be noted that no mention has been made of "liking" or "judging" as elements in aesthetic experience. This is because neither is a proper component of aesthetic experience. It is a very common idea that what one is supposed to do when confronted with a work of art is to evaluate it; to decide whether it is any good, and even more im-portantly, whether one "likes" it or not. So people often go around an art exhibit as they would go around a smorgasbord table, sampling a bit of this and that and saying "I like that one. No, this one I don't like. Oh, I love that one. This one I don't care for at all." The snap judgment is a function of "snap perception" and "snap reaction." Few people are capable of an instantaneous, deep, sophisticated perception of and re-sponse to an art work's complexities. In the vast majority of cases quick judgments reflect a superficial level of aesthetic experience.

But more important than that, the idea that one's experience of art should be one of liking or judging actually *gets in the way* of aesthetic experience. Aesthetic perception should be unhindered by concern about judgment-making. It should be a free, open, uncluttered giving up of oneself to the aesthetic qualities being regarded. The less concerned one is about having to decide about the "goodness" of the work one is at-tending to, the more likely one is of being able to share openly and fully in its aesthetic qualities. And the less worried one is about one's own subjective evaluation of the work the more can one's reaction consist of a sharing of the expressiveness of the perceived qualities. Aesthetic reac-tion should consist of what aesthetic perception causes. It should *not* con-sist of something brought in as an extraneous factor, for this only prevents fresh, direct reaction to the expressive content of the work.

Art does not exist in order to be "liked," in the sense of providing simple, transitory pleasures. It makes sense to "like" vanilla ice cream better than chocolate, or to "like" peaches better than plums. Concern about "liking" art usually puts it on that superficial level. Art contains insights to be shared; it offers self-knowledge of a very basic sort. This is true of simple as well as complex art. The way to share art's power is to aesthetically experience it—not to taste it to find out whether it pleases the palate. Yet it is this latter, superficial kind of experience which teachers actively promote when they constantly ask "Did you like this song?" "Did you like this painting?" "Did you like this poem?" As if it *mattered!* What matters is, "Did you hear what happened in this song and did you feel what you heard?" "Did you see more in this painting and did you feel more of what you saw?" "Did you grasp more of the subtleties of this poem and did you feel more subtly as a result?" In the sense of perceiving more and reacting more, the central question is "Did you *understand?*"

> . . . art, like science, is a mental activity whereby we bring certain contents of the world into the realm of objectively valid cognition . . . it is the particular office of art to do this with the world's emotional content. According to this view,

therefore, the function of art is not to give the percipient any pleasure, however noble, but to acquaint him with something which he has not known before. Art, just like science, aims primarily to be "understood." Whether that understanding which art transmits then pleases the feeling percipient, whether it leaves him indifferent or elicits repugnance, is of no significance to art as pure art. But since that of which it makes us aware is always of an emotive character, it normally calls forth, more or less peremptorily, a reaction of pleasure or displeasure in the perceiving subject. This explains quite readily how the erroneous opinion has arisen that the percipient's delight and assent are the criteria of art.[4]

When art is experienced aesthetically and understood aesthetically, it delights in a way that few experiences in human life provide. To share *that* delight, which is the delight of understanding more fully the nature of human reality, is the important job of aesthetic education. In talking about the literary form of "tragedy," Susanne Langer says,

Few people know why tragedy is a source of deep satisfaction; they invent all sorts of psychological explanations, from emotional catharsis to a sense of superiority because the hero's misfortunes are not one's own. But the real source is the joy of revelation, the vision of a world wholly significant, of life spending itself and death the signature of its completion. It is simply the joy of great art, which is the perception of created form wholly expressive, that is to say, beautiful.[5]

To share the joy of art—the perception of expressive form—one must help people experience art aesthetically, free from the strictures of liking or judging. Let judgments come later, as reflection, after the fact, about particular aesthetic experiences. Aesthetic education can and must help such reflection be sensible, and therefore to promote better aesthetic experiences for the future. But such reflection, including the self-analysis of "liking" or "disliking," should be purged from aesthetic experience itself.

If, as has been suggested, the major goal of aesthetic education is to improve the ability of all people to have aesthetic experiences; that is, to heighten all people's aesthetic sensitivity, how would music education contribute to this goal? Again we ask the central question of this book: How can music education be aesthetic education?

---

4 Otto Baensch, "Art and Feeling," in *Reflections on Art,* ed. Susanne K. Langer (New York: Oxford University Press, 1961), pp. 10, 11.

5 Langer, *Feeling and Form,* p. 405.

First, music education must use musical works which are capable of being aesthetically perceived and aesthetically reacted to. It should not be assumed, however, that every piece of music should be so simple that *all* of its aesthetic qualities can be perceived by the children studying it, listening to it, performing it. Good works of art are likely to contain so much expressiveness that few people will perceive all possible subtleties and complexities. Partial understanding is probably the rule rather than the exception. If one accepts the fact that not all of a work is likely to be perceived one can use music of a much more sophisticated sort than if one assumes that all music must be so simple that every child can get every bit of its musical quality. Of course some reasonable balance is needed, but errors of the past seem to have been in the direction of over-simplicity and therefore of minimal excitement and minimal involvement. It is time to be bolder about musical materials—not disregarding the age and experience of students, but not underestimating their capacities or their willingness to accept aesthetic challenge.

Second, teaching and learning must be arranged so that aesthetic experiencing is central and all other matters play a supporting role. Every possible opportunity must be provided for aesthetic perception to take place in contexts which encourage, or, at the least, allow for aesthetic reaction to occur. Music education, for many people, consists of material learned and skills gained. It is being suggested here that music education should consist of musical aesthetic experiences. Of course reading, writing, practicing, talking, testing, are legitimate and necessary components of music education. But when they become separated from musical experience itself they have become separated from that which provides their primary reason for existence.

In the "study" part of music education—the part used in the service of deepening aesthetic experiences of music—attention should be focused on that which, if perceived, can arouse aesthetic reaction. Conditions of sound which are expressive can be revealed to children of all ages. The primary responsibility of music education, at every level and in every part of the program, is to reveal more fully the musical conditions which should be perceived and felt. The qualities of sound which make sound expressive—melody, harmony, rhythm, tone color, texture, form—are the objective "data" with which music teachers systematically deal. Illuminating these "data" in musical settings is the primary task of musical learning.

Such illumination requires, in addition to the handling of musical stuff itself through analyzing, performing, and composing, conceptualization about that which is to be perceived. Conception is a major means for developing perception. And, in turn, increased perception deepens conception. A constant interaction between conception about expressive qualities of music, and perception of those qualities, should pervade every aspect of musical study. This requires a careful use of language, because language is the indispensable mode of conceptualization. Language becomes a powerful tool for increasing aesthetic sensitivity when it is devoted to the refinement of aesthetic perception, in contexts which present perception as an integral part of expressive music to be felt. The music program is the means for systematically arranging for aesthetic perception and aesthetic reaction—aesthetic experience—to take place.

QUESTIONS FOR DISCUSSION

1. What natural phenomena, in addition to those named in the chapter, exhibit the qualities of "livingness," and therefore seem pervaded with significance?

2. Why can the position about aesthetic experience being taken in this book be said to be a "naturalistic" or "biologically-based" one? How is this position different from or similar to the old idea that "art is an imitation of nature"?

3. What common meanings can you identify among the words used to describe the characteristics of aesthetic experience: "intrinsicality," "disinterestedness," "psychical distance," "empathy," "tension in repose," "immediate," "direct," "involvement in expressive form," "aesthetic attitude?"

4. Try to think of examples other than those given to illustrate the differences among scientific, practical, religious, and aesthetic experiences (and any other kinds you care to add). Use prototype people (scientist, farmer, etc.) in various situations. In each example, concentrate on 1) the type of perception, and 2) the resulting reaction.

5. Are you willing to call experiences of scientific discovery, or satisfaction about a job well done, or thinking through a problem to its conclusion, "aesthetic experiences"? Or would you prefer to call them something else and add that they may very well contain aesthetic quality?

6. In what sense can aesthetic experience be said to be "creative"? What are similarities and differences from the creativity of composing or performing?

7. What are some dangers of thinking that aesthetic experiences are rare in life; reserved for certain types of people; not for children; available only from masterworks?

8. What advantages for developing the ability to have aesthetic experiences might accrue from avoiding "liking" and "judging" as elements in aesthetic experience? How might discussions of preferences and judgments serve to enhance aesthetic sensitivity?

9. Give tangible examples for music education of the principles that 1) music capable of arousing aesthetic experience be used, 2) aesthetic experience of music be central and other matters peripheral, 3) study should concentrate on that which can arouse aesthetic experience, 4) conceptualization can be a major aid in developing aesthetic sensitivity if properly used.

SUPPLEMENTARY READINGS

1. Broudy, Harry S., "The Structure of Knowledge in the Arts," in *Education and the Structure of Knowledge,* ed. Stanley Elam. Chicago: Rand Mc-Nally & Company, 1964, pp. 75–106. Also in *Aesthetics and Criticism in Art Education,* ed. Ralph A. Smith. Chicago: Rand McNally & Company, 1966, pp. 23–45. This essay would also be appropriate as a supplementary reading for Chapter Five. It is listed here because of its rich implications for developing aesthetic perceptivity.

2. Dewey, John, *Art as Experience.* New York: Capricorn Books, 1958, Chapter 1, "The Live Creature" and Chapter 3, "Having an Experience." These two chapters are directly concerned with aesthetic experience and have been extremely influential on modern notions of what constitutes aesthetic experience.

3. Langer, Susanne K., *Feeling and Form.* New York: Charles Scribner's Sons, 1953. Chapter 4, "Semblance," is a penetrating discussion of the "illusion" presented by art works for aesthetic experiencing. Chapter 21, "The Work and Its Public" contains some of Langer's most direct statements about aesthetic experience, as well as some thoughts about aesthetic education.

4. Langer, Susanne K., *Problems of Art.* New York: Charles Scribner's Sons, 1957, Chapter 4, "Living Form." The ideas presented in this chapter are developed in *Mind: An Essay On Human Feeling,* but are more easily accessible here.

5. Schoen, Max, *Art and Beauty.* New York: The Macmillan Company, 1932, Chapter 6, "The Experience of Beauty," especially pp. 133–149. An old but still very useful treatment of various views of aesthetic experience.

CHAPTER SEVEN

musical meaning and musical experience

The position about art being taken in this book is, essentially, a "musical" one. The assertion that all the arts should be approached as expressive forms, perceived as expressive forms, responded to as expressive forms, judged as expressive forms, taught as expressive forms, is an assertion heavily colored by a musical outlook toward art. Of all the arts music can be most purely expressive, unmixed with symbol matter of any sort. The presentation of aesthetic qualities in a self-sufficient, self-complete way can be more easily achieved in music than in other arts, which often require a context of conventional symbols against which or through which the aesthetic expressiveness is presented. This does not in any way mean that music is therefore the "best" or the "highest" or the "purest" art (although music educators often and understandably assume this to be a self-evident truth), but simply that the peculiar nature of sound lends itself very naturally to totally aesthetic use. Walter Pater acknowledged this fact in one of the most famous (and most misquoted) statements ever made about music as the most "artistic" art (the famous sentence is italicized—by Pater—in the following excerpt):

> . . . music [is] the typical, or ideally consummate art, the object of the great *Anders-streben* of all art, of all that is artistic, or partakes of artistic qualities. *All art constantly aspires towards the condition of music.* For while in all other kinds of art it is possible to distinguish the matter [symbol] from the form, and the understanding can always make this distinction, yet it is the constant effort of art to obliterate it. That the mere matter of a poem, for instance, its subject, namely, its given incidents or situation—that the mere matter of a picture, the actual circumstances of an event, the actual topography of a landscape—should be nothing without the form, the spirit, of the handling, that this form, this mode of handling, should become an end in itself, should penetrate every part of the matter: this is what all art constantly strives after, and achieves in different degrees.[1]

Every art work which achieves the status of an expressive form is successful to some degree as art. The old argument as to whether the presence of non-artistic material increases or decreases the impact of the work as aesthetic need not be belabored. What is of importance is the recognition that the aesthetic qualities of things are what have aesthetic value. Under the assumption that it will be helpful to aesthetic educators to more fully understand how aesthetic qualities function, an investigation of how music functions aesthetically should be of use to teachers of all the arts and especially to teachers of music.[2]

Many ideas about musical experience and musical meaning have been implied in the preceding chapters. The major ideas can now be made explicit. The following diagram will help focus our discussion.

While the number of actual experiences of music is doubtlessly as large as the number of people who have ever responded to music, broad categories of common experiences can be identified. The categories listed below are conceived very broadly, as guidelines for discussion, rather than as an exhaustive, rigid framework into which all possible musical experiences must fit. Also, as with all complex human behaviors, in-

---

[1] Walter Pater, *The Renaissance* (London: Macmillan and Co., Limited, 1910), pp. 134–35.

[2] That the art of music is regarded by Susanne K. Langer as the touchstone art for understanding all art makes her writings particularly relevant for music education. This is one important reason for the influence of her writings on this book and for her extensive influence on music education at the level of philosophy and, increasingly, at the level of practice.

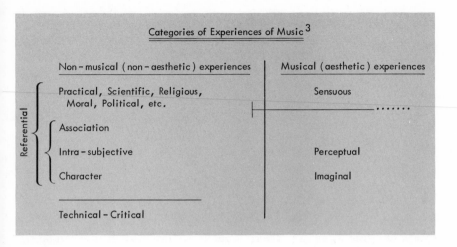

Categories of Experiences of Music [3]

Non – musical (non – aesthetic) experiences	Musical (aesthetic) experiences
Practical, Scientific, Religious, Moral, Political, etc.	Sensuous
Association	
Intra – subjective	Perceptual
Character	Imaginal
Technical – Critical	

(Referential)

stances of "pure" experiences unmixed with bits and pieces of others are probably the exception rather than the rule. Nevertheless, it is helpful to map out large areas of experience in order to provide a manageable structure upon which ideas can be organized.

The non-musical experiences are so called because they are not based on the two necessary components of any experience which can be called "aesthetic": aesthetic perception and aesthetic reaction. For an aesthetic experience to be a musical aesthetic experience the perception must be of the asethetic qualities of sound and the reaction must be caused by the expressiveness of those qualities. None of the responses in the left-hand column fulfill these conditions.

The practical, scientific, religious, moral, political, etc. experiences of music are not a function of musical qualities of sound which are inherently expressive *as music.* At a political rally, for example, a candidate's theme-song might be played before he appears at the podium. The song is perceived as a symbol of candidate "X," who has propounded an exciting policy for improving American government. Perceived for its designation the song is reacted to appropriately—with stirrings of pride, hope, dedication to American ideals. The song will probably be of a generally exciting sort suitable to its purpose of arousing excitement for the candidate, but the embodied, expressive, insightful, created, presentational, unconsummated meanings (p. 60) of the sounds as aesthetically

---

[3] Several of these terms have been adapted from the studies described in Max Schoen, *Art and Beauty* (New York: The Macmillan Company, 1932), Chapter VII, "Beauty in Music."

organized (expressively formed) are quite peripheral to the experience if they are present at all. The song is a symbol; perceived and reacted to as such. Certainly the song is fulfilling a legitimate and important function. That function, however, is not primarily an aesthetic one.

The other experiences listed along with "political" each exhibit the same characteristics of symbols—perceived as designating something outside the sounds themselves and reacted to according to what is designated. Music, as the other arts, has served such conventionally symbolic functions throughout history and continues to do so. There is no reason why music should not serve such functions. They are important to society in a variety of ways. Indeed, it is difficult to conceive many social occasions without music as a functional component. But the position being taken in this book is that music education should be primarily *music* education; that is, education for the aesthetic, or musical, qualities and values of music as an art. There is really no problem in understanding music's functional, non-aesthetic uses and the values of such uses. These values are self-evident. The nature and value of music *as art,* on the other hand, is a complex matter requiring systematic explanation. If music education makes any claim at all to being *musical* education—to being *aesthetic* education—it is necessary to have a philosophy which explains the musical, aesthetic nature and value of music. One important aspect of that explanation is to distinguish between experiences of music which are musical and those which are not.

The Association, Intra-subjective and Character responses are somewhat different from the practical, scientific, etc. responses in that they are not functional in the same way as the latter. In the Association experience the music suggests any number of extra-musical ideas or occurrences in the life of the responder. A typical statement describing such an experience might be "The music reminded me of when I was a child, and we went swimming at the beach, and a storm came up and the waves became dangerous." Or, "I kept thinking about my term paper on Mozart, and how I would have to work on it after the concert." Or, "As soon as the music started I thought about how I got my first teaching job and had to start a chorus and a band at the same time, and we performed this piece at the first concert." The music in such experiences serves as a stimulus for memories, worries, self-conversations of all sorts. The sounds of the music get the experience going, but they are not perceived and responded to for their embodied expressiveness. The music fades from consciousness, providing a pleasant background against which to daydream.

The Intra-subjective experience is an Association experience in which the visual or literary imagination is stirred by the music. Rather than calling up a particular association from one's life the Intra-subjective response calls up all sorts of fanciful images. A person might say "I thought of a beautiful forest, with the sun shining through the trees, and butterflies and birds were flying here and there." Or, "I began to make up a story, with a prince and princess and witches and monsters." Or, "It was a parade, and the bands came by and there were floats and balloons and riders on horseback."[4] Again, the music stimulates a great deal of mental activity, but this activity is only remotely related to what is actually going on in the music.

The Character response focuses on the "mood" or "character" element of music. "It was very depressing. I felt that death was all around and all life must come to an end." Or, "How happy it made me. I wanted to smile at the whole world." Or, "This movement is dainty. The last one was soulful. I wonder what the next one will be." Here the most obvious mood-quality of the music causes the response, with no grasp of the expressiveness of the musical events beyond the superficial level of emotional designation.

Experience of program music and vocal music include elements of all the responses described so far, either singly or in various combinations. As has been stated many times in our explanation of how art works can contain conventional symbols, the program or the words can enter into the aesthetic expressiveness of a piece when they become immersed in the expressiveness of the melody, harmony, rhythm, etc. When this occurs the experience is musical (aesthetic) even though a non-musical (non-aesthetic) component is present. The descriptions given above of the non-musical responses to music assume that they remain at a non-aesthetic level, as they often do. Similarly for program or vocal music. Such music can be experienced aesthetically, of course, but our interest at the moment is in the (very common) non-aesthetic experiences of this music.

Non-musical experiences of music—regardless of what kind of music —are closely related to one another and probably can be separated only artificially. They are natural responses, occurring spontaneously, with no necessity for musical training or perceptual development of any sort. Because music is perceived and responded to as either 1) a symbol of something non-musical, or 2) an occasion for non-musical reminiscence or fantasy-making, there is little one can do to "improve" or "educate" such responses. Of course the teacher can encourage such responses by asking all sorts of non-musical questions about music, such as "What do

---

4 The Walt Disney movie *Fantasia* gave some clear examples of Intra-subjective interpretations of music, in wide-screen, stereophonic, technicolor gloriousness.

you think it means?" "What does it make you imagine?" "How does it make you feel?" "Can you tell a story appropriate to this music?" "Does it make you remember anything that has happened to you?" "Is this music sad or happy; like this painting or like this other painting; like a sunny day or a rainy day; blue or red; like butterflies or like elephants; heroic or cowardly; etc. etc. etc.?" All such questions will effectively call attention away from the music itself to matters referred to by the music. They will therefore force the experience of music to be non-musical, and, even more importantly, *teach people that non-musical responses to music are appropriate and desirable.* In this, such "teaching" does educate. If one is not a Referentialist, but instead is an Absolutist, one can only say that such "teaching" can only mis-educate.

Music education has been and is now to some degree *non-music* education. A stronger way to state it would be *anti-music* education. When teachers foster non-musical experiences of music, when they give the impression that such experiences are what music is essentially for, when they prevent aesthetic experiences of music from taking place (let alone *helping* aesthetic experiences to take place), they are being non-music educators and are producing non-musical people. This may not be an "immediate and present danger" to people or society, but it certainly is little help to people, society, or music. All non-music education does is to get in the way of music education. But if music education is as important for human life as our philosophy has suggested, non-music education becomes a serious obstacle to the development of an important component—the aesthetic component—of people's lives. That *is* a serious matter and a most unfortunate one. Of all people music educators should not be the ones to weaken the power of music to be musically experienced.

Some people have the idea that non-musical experiences are appropriate for younger children and can be phased out as the children grow older. What this says, in effect, is, "Let us make sure that we start children out on the wrong foot. Let us teach them, at the most impressionable time of their lives, that music is not an art, that they should experience music non-musically, that the more non-musical they become now the more likely it is they will become musical 'later.' Let us prevent children from sharing the aesthetic joy and aesthetic delight and aesthetic significance which music can add to life, for life begins 'later.' Aesthetic experience is not for children: let us teach accordingly. Our non-aesthetic use of music will eventually lead to music as it 'really is.' How? Somehow."

This attitude, all too common in music education and in art education generally, has no doubt done more to block the growth of aesthetic sensitivity than any other single thing in education. If anything at all is known about how people learn, it is that people learn to do what they do. Teach children non-aesthetically and they will learn to be non-aesthetic. Teach them aesthetically, and they will learn, to the level of whatever capacity they have, to be more aesthetically sensitive. If music education is to be aesthetic education it must be, first of all, *music* education. It cannot be so if it fosters non-musical experiences of music.

The Technical-Critical experience of music is separated from the Referential experiences because it is different in kind even though it is, in and of itself, a non-aesthetic experience. In this response the perception is of the technical and peripheral elements which go into the making of music and the reaction is a function of that kind of perception: "What a bright string tone this orchestra has. It's perfect for this piece but the Mahler needs more depth." "That soprano certainly has trouble in her upper register." "Did you notice how the conductor used his right hand for some of the cues?" "I heard this pianist several years ago and his style has changed a great deal since then." "The sound on this recording is blurry." "The auditorium isn't very full. I wonder if it will affect the tone quality."

An endless number of such responses surrounds musical activity in all its aspects. Much of this kind of perception is directly applicable to the development of perception which is aesthetic. By itself it is "pre-aesthetic" but when used as a means to aesthetic ends is a necessary aspect of musical education. One of the major occupational hazards of being a professional musician, music teacher, or music student, is that one can easily become so concerned about the techniques and apparatus of musical activity that one seldom has enough "psychical distance" to be able to experience music aesthetically. This is too bad, but at least the professional can gain solace from the fact that he is being paid (or will be paid) for his expertise, and that if he is sometimes too busy being an expert to enjoy the music this is part of the game. There is no such excuse, however, for focusing so heavily on the Technical-Critical level of experience that children are not able to go beyond it to the aesthetic experience of music. Many people get the impression from their musical education that the Technical-Critical response is the "really musical" way to experience music. This is an understandable result of the common and unfortunate separation in music education of technical learnings from musical aesthetic experiences.

Musical experiences of music are so because they consist of perception of the aesthetic qualities of music (including non-aesthetic elements if they are present) and reaction to the expressiveness of those qualities. The Sensuous response is represented as an open-ended continuum because its range extends from the non-musical (or minimally musical) to musical responses of a sophistication not yet fully explored or understood. In the Sensuous response music is perceived for its surface sound-qualities with little if any attention to the inner organization and interrelation of the sounds. Rather than listening with a perceptive ear for coherent events one listens "with the skin," the immediate sound itself—its surface texture and intensity and color—being not so much "heard" as "felt."

All experiences of music, ranging from the most naively non-musical to the most deeply musical, include the sensuous element, for sound is always "felt" whether or not it is really "heard." But while the sensuous element is a necessary component of all experiences of music it can be and often is the dominant if not the exclusive level of response. At the non-musical end of the continuum the sensuous experience is a mindless, undiscerning, passive wallowing in the sheer existence of sound. The sound can be the driving, hypnotic beat of rock and roll, overwhelming in primitiveness and volume, entering the pores more than the ears, vibrating every muscle (many of which oldsters have not used in years) and blotting out everything but sound-sense. But it can also be equally mindless while not so earthy, as when those no longer young find their own (more restrained) physical pleasure in the tickle of Lawrence Welk's bubbling sounds, or the soothing balm of Mantovani's shimmering strings, sparkling brasses, glistening woodwinds. The "kicks" in both cases are sensuous ones, minimally musical because perception is minimal, but very attractive and pleasant because sensuality is, after all, a basic human characteristic.

Bathing in warm sound is so popular a pastime (the temperature of the sound simply cools down as age advances) that a whole industry exists to supply "music to be comforted by." There is nothing wrong with such use of music except for the impression it gives that all musical experience should be soporific in its effects. This tense world is so overlayed with soothing Muzak that one feels, occasionally, as if he is constantly wading through aural molasses. The teenager plugged in through the ear to a transistor radio is sucking on a pacifier but in a socially acceptable way. All of this use of sound for creature comfort no doubt fills a human need, but it does make it more difficult for the music educator to use music for quite the opposite purpose; that is, to help people feel more sensitively rather than less so.

It is paradoxical, then, that the Sensuous response to music can be powerfully aesthetic, requiring high levels of perception and reaction. As one moves along the continuum from mindless immersion in indiscriminate sound to subtle, complex, expressive uses of the sensuous qualities of music, one enters a seemingly endless realm of aesthetic meaning embodied in the surface impact of sound. All important music, no matter when composed, depends for at least part of its expressiveness on the sensuousness of tone, and it is one of the major responsibilities of music education to help people become more sensitive to this dimension of musical affect. The means for doing so are the same as for all musical education: helping people perceive the conditions of sound which are expressive (in this case sensuously expressive) in contexts which encourage feelingful reactions to what is perceived. No matter what type of music is being used, no matter what the age of the students, no matter what the activity—singing, playing, composing, listening, etc.—musical learning will include some attention to the sensuous level of aesthetic responsiveness.

One of the most interesting and most puzzling facts of contemporary life is that in the aesthetic use of the arts the sensuous level of expressiveness has expanded enormously in a very short time. In the past the sensuous component was just that—a component part of an aesthetic presentation which was organized to be perceived for its interrelated properties, presented through a sensuous medium. Now, in practically every mode of art, the sensuous has been used as the total aesthetic presentation, with no intrinsic interrelations of aesthetic properties (or no *perceivable* interrelations at any rate) to be regarded as "meaningful" in the sense of coherent, related, structured, interconnected. Aleatory (chance, random) art, or art so structured that it gives the impression of randomness, such as so-called "total serialization" in music (4, Chapter 5 and Part III) has no content of perceivable interrelated aesthetic events, and so must be responded to at the sheerly sensuous level and is usually intended to be responded to that way. But far from being a mindless, passive kind of response, this level of sensuous experience can be extremely active and perceptive.

It will no doubt take many years and thousands of pages of writing (one shudders to think of how many more grimly technical, humorless articles remain to be written on the subject) to begin to resolve the question of whether the sheerly sensuous level of response can be "meaningful" as music has been and is when the sensuous is part of a tonal matrix which contains some sort of structure. Opinions on this matter range from total advocacy, as in John Cage's *Silence,*[5] to thoroughgoing skepticism, as in the writings of Leonard B. Meyer (especially 4). The obligations of music education in this controversy are 1) to remain open to the debate, not letting tradition or prejudice alone decide the matter, but weighing the pros and cons and not expecting simple, yes or no

---

[5] (Middletown, Connecticut: Wesleyan University Press, 1961.)

answers, and 2) to seriously consider the effects on the vigor of musical culture of shutting children off from one of the most interesting controversies in the history of art. There is no need for music educators to take a "position" about *avant garde* music (aleatory or otherwise), but there is a serious need for an open, free, non-prejudicial sharing with people of all the musical opportunities, puzzling as well as safe, which one's times make available.

The Perceptual and Imaginal levels of musical experience apply to all music, past and present, except that very small portion of recent music which is sheerly sensuous in content. The Perceptual response includes 1) perception, to some degree, of the constituent elements of music—melody, harmony, rhythm, etc., including any non-musical material which might be present—and their interrelations, and their use in the context of a particular style, and 2) reaction to the expressiveness of the perceived musical (and non-musical) material. This, obviously, is the response which has been called "aesthetic experience" throughout this book. In musical terms it is a matter of perceiving, for example, the contour of a melody, the relation of the melody to its harmony, the rhythmic structure of both, the tone color of the presentation, the function the melody and harmony serve in the developing form. But this kind of perception is far from being the coldy clinical "ear-training" which characterizes the Technical-Critical response. The perception is itself *feelingful* perception, in which the musical events are experienced, first and foremost, as *expressive* events.

When musical perception becomes separated from musical reaction the experience is pre-aesthetic or non-aesthetic. When musical reaction is caused by other things than musical perception the experience is, again, pre-aesthetic or non-aesthetic. The old, belabored distinction between the so-called "intellectual" (perceptive) and "emotional" (reactive) components of aesthetic experience is a fruitless and misleading one, for when experience is genuinely aesthetic the two become indistinguishable.

The Perceptual response, then, is a "reactively perceptive" one. Some people, especially highly trained musicians, may tend to consciously identify the actual musical devices which are used to create expressiveness. ("Here comes the deceptive cadence—now we go to the authentic.") The amount of conscious "naming" which accompanies musical perception and reaction will range from very much to none at all, depending on the background and/or personality of the listener. But it is extremely important to understand that musical perception in no way depends on the ability to name the technical devices which cause musical expressiveness. What must be perceived, *whether or not it can be named,* is the uncertainty of the movement through that deceptive cadence and the resolution of the movement in an authentic cadence. Being able to name the device employed is extremely helpful, but as a means toward the end of making the expressiveness of the device more available for experiencing.

The Imaginal response to music is an extension of the Perceptual response. It includes, in addition to the perception of expressive musical events and the reaction to the perceived expressiveness, a constant anticipation of musical events. The experience is marked by an absorption in the way the music sets up expectations, deviates from expected resolutions, causes uncertainty in modes of continuation, delays expected consequences of events, satisfies musical implications. The listener not only perceives the melody in relation to its harmony, for example, but anticipates changes in the movement of the melody and the harmonic changes which seem to be implied. He feels the section coming to a close, anticipating a cadence which will mark the end of one section and imply the beginning of another, noticing the unexpected treatment of the movement toward the cadence, the expressive diversions, the sudden fulfillment, the much-expected new melodic idea but with a surprising carryover of harmony from the previous section. His musical perception and musical reaction are brought to bear in such a way that he is, in a sense, *creating along with the music.* He is absorbed in the world of expressive sound, both molding the experience by his active participation and being molded by the events as they interact with his expectations. There is a sense of "oneness" with the music—of being submerged in expressiveness while at the same time influencing the amount and quality of expressiveness gained.

The Perceptual and Imaginal responses, obviously, are intense, active, extremely attentive responses, engaging both mind and feelings together at high levels of concentration. This is worlds apart from the "let's relax to the music" kind of response so common inside and outside of educational settings. If one is to share the insights into human subjectivity presented by the aesthetic qualities of sound, however, one must share them in the only way they *can* be shared—by becoming absorbed in them with one's power's of thinking and feeling.

The analysis of musical experience given here implies a theory of how sound can be used to give rise to "meaning." For the Referentialist musical sounds produce "meaning" in the same way that any symbolisms produce meaning, so there is little problem in explaining how music is "meaningful." The Formalist denies any need for explaining how sounds become meaningful because "sounds mean themselves," and there the discussion ends. The Expressionist is in the position of having to explain precisely how tonal events are experienced as containing "meaning"; how sounds can present conditions which are perceived and responded to as expressive of subjective reality. How, in short, does sound function aesthetically?

The clearest and most extensive explanation of the processes by which sound can be organized to produce expressiveness is that given by Leonard B. Meyer (3). With many examples and detailed analyses Meyer shows how tonal events arouse tendencies, cause expectations, produce various kinds and degrees of tendency-resolutions and expectation-satisfactions. When a system of sound-relationships—a piece of music—is experienced aesthetically, the tonal matrix of tensions and resolutions produces tensions and resolutions within the experiencer, and these are "significant" because they are analagous to the modes of human feeling. As Susanne Langer explains:

> The tonal structures we call "music" bear a close logical similarity to the forms of human feeling—forms of growth and attenuation, flowing and stowing, conflict and resolution, speed, arrest, terrific excitement, calm, or subtle activation and dreamy lapses—not joy and sorrow perhaps, but the poignancy of either and both—the greatness and brevity and eternal passing of everything vitally felt. Such is the pattern, or logical form, of sentience; and the pattern of music is that same form worked out in pure, measured sound and silence. Music is a tonal analogue of emotive life.[6]

For technical explanations of how rhythm, melody, harmony, form, etc. produce the conditions of affect, the reader should explore *Emotion and Meaning in Music,* especially Chapters III–VII. Two implications from Meyer's treatment of musical meaningfulness are so relevant to music education that attention to them is warranted at this point. The first has to do with the necessity of correct style expectations. The second concerns the matter of bases for judging the quality of music.

In order for sounds to have tendencies—to arouse expectations that certain things are likely to happen—and in order for musical tendencies to be manipulated in expressive ways by deviations, delays, resolutions, uncertainties, etc., a context must exist which provides people with a commonly accepted sphere of musical probabilities. Such a sphere of probabilities, in which a recognizable degree of predictability exists, is called a "style." When melody, rhythm, harmony, tone color, texture, form are used in characteristic ways, so that some unity of expectation is

---

[6] Langer, *Feeling and Form,* p. 27.

possible on the part of the perceiver, a style is in operation, providing the basic set of agreed-upon "likelihoods" for musical sharing to be built upon.

Trying to respond musically to sounds in an unknown style is like watching a game being played in which none of the rules or regulations or purposes are known to the person watching. One tries one's best to make some "sense" out of the proceedings, both in the music and the game, but unless some probabilities are discovered—some organizing factors which provide the possibility for perceiving relationships—the experience can only be "meaningless." No sharing can take place because perception is nonexistent and reaction is therefore impossible (except the reaction of frustration).

A great deal of music is meaningless to a great many people (and therefore frustrating to them) because they are ignorant of the music's "style"; that is, they can not perceive and react to the aural events as being coherent, interrelated, unified, "sensible." Eastern music (by which is *not* meant the Tokyo Philharmonic playing Mozart's 40th) is largely unaccessible to the casual Western listener, faddish dabbling in "exotic music" notwithstanding. Jazz is a closed book to many concert-music lovers and much concert (or "classical") music is meaningless to many jazz enthusiasts. Music of past eras in Western culture has little or no meaning for some people, and much contemporary music makes no sense to a great many listeners. Truly, the "universality" of musical sharing is more a fond hope than a reality.

Unfortunately, music education has often contributed to musical parochialism by emphasizing certain musical styles (those in "good standing") and neglecting—sometimes *ignoring*—certain others. This is especially true in the musical education of young children, where musical experiences have often been limited to music which the children can sing, thus narrowing the field to the style of simple diatonicism and even, more recently, to music using the pentatonic scale. Serious thought must be given to the dangers of such restricted acquaintance with musical style at the very age when tastes are being formed and long-lasting impressions are being made.[7] This raises the question of how much reliance should be placed on performance as the major mode of musical education, a question which will be touched upon in the following chapters. At this point it would seem clear that anything which restricts rather

---

[7] For some comments about the importance of an early introduction to complex contemporary music, see (4), p. 274–76.

than widens a familiarity with the rich diversity of musical styles available to people should be regarded with suspicion, or, at the least, compensated for by other means of providing musical experiences.

The notion that children—of *any* age—should be "protected" from certain styles, these usually being the more puzzling contemporary styles, is one which a more mature profession would find intolerable. A two-pronged obligation is involved here; one to children, who deserve the richest, most diverse possible musical fare; and the other to music itself, which deserves, at the very least, that those who are dedicated to a fuller sharing of the art not inadvertently produce people with restricted tastes, built-in prejudices, provincial preferences. The surest ways to keep musical options open, to encourage wide-ranging musical interests and widely varying musical pleasures, are 1) to display in all that is done at every stage of music education a joyous, open, free acceptance of good music in many styles, and 2) to systematically help people share more of the many musical styles by skillful teaching which shows how music is expressive no matter what its style. This implies a concentration on 1) those components of sound used in all styles, such as dynamics, tempo, the various media for producing sounds, pitch direction, register, range, rhythmic patterns, pace, consonance and dissonance, phrase structure, variety, repetition, etc., and 2) how the pervasive, expressive modes of sound are used in characteristic ways in each different style. Good music teaching—*musical* music teaching—will include such concerns as the background for all activities at every grade level.

The question of how the quality of music can be ascertained is, of course, a very old and complex one, a full treatment of which would be beyond the scope of this book. However, our explanation of musical experience and the theory of musical meaning on which it is based suggest the broad outlines for a functional approach to musical evaluation which can be of use to teachers as they choose music for any level of the music education program. For, whether or not music educators care to think of themselves as "arbiters of taste," an inevitable degree of control over musical experiences does exist and always will exist so long as formal teaching and learning of music takes place. It is impossible to avoid making value judgments about music when one deals with music as a professional. And while any overt imposition of musical values would be distasteful to most music educators and most students, the entire music education enterprise is built on the assumption that musical tastes can be improved, that musical experiences can be deepened, that musical enjoyment can be refined, that musical significance can be made more available to all people. These assumptions, all of which are very healthy and beyond criticism, do imply a movement toward "better" musical experiences of "better" music. The question is, what makes music "better"?

Two aspects of musical "goodness" can be identified as the bases on which value-judgments can be made. (4, Chapter 2).[8] The first, which can be termed "excellence," has to do with the level of syntactical or structural refinement in the music. To the extent that the construction of a piece of music—whether a simple song or a complex symphony—is marked by qualities of skillfulness, expertness, competence, aptness, consistency of style, clarity of basic intent, sufficient complexity and variety for its scope, adroitness, inventiveness, craftsmanship, the piece can reasonably be judged to be "better" than one which is lacking in these qualities (a lack of any of them would imply the presence of its opposite —incompetence, inconsistency, etc.). Because musical affect is a function of the musical tendencies, resistances, delays, diversions, expectations, resolutions, inhibitions, etc. presented by tonal events, the excellence of construction of these events is a fundamental basis for judging the "goodness" of a piece. The notion of musical excellence as one basis for choosing "good music" can be of immediate use to the practicing music educator.

But important as syntactical excellence is as a component of good music it is not sufficient for judging musical quality. A second aspect of value must be included. This, which can be termed "greatness," has to do with the level of profundity of the music's expressive content. To the extent that the conditions of expressiveness in a particular piece are capable of producing deep, abiding insights into the nature of subjective reality that piece can be called "great." To the extent that a particular composer achieves the level of greatness in his works he can be considered a great composer. As has been suggested in several places in this book, an art work which succeeds in capturing a sense of the life of feeling in its aesthetic content can be considered to be a "good" work. Greatness occurs when the sense of feelingfulness is so striking, so "true," so revealing of the nature of the subjective human condition, that one who experiences the work's impact feels changed in the direction of a deeper understanding of what it is like to be human. Certainly the experiencer must be *capable* of sharing such insights, bringing to the music the aesthetic sensitivity which will enable him to perceive keenly and react deeply. The major objective of music education is to develop, to what-

---

8 For a more extended discussion of Meyer's conception of musical value and its implications for music education, see Bennett Reimer, "Leonard Meyer's Theory of Value and Greatness in Music," *Journal of Research in Music Education*, X, No. 2 (Fall, 1962).

ever extent is possible, every person's capacity to share the deepest levels of musical greatness. For the more of the qualities of greatness that a person can experience the more can his sense of "humanness" be refined.

It is quite obvious to anyone who has ever tried to judge the quality of a work of art that no absolute scale of excellence or greatness exists. Excellence is somewhat easier to evaluate than greatness because there is a larger element of objectivity in the realm of syntactical craftsmanship. Greatness is difficult to judge because the quality of greatness is always more than the sum of its syntactical parts. Even if one could "add up" the amount of structural excellence in a piece the level of greatness would not necessarily be equal to the level of excellence. Some works achieve a high order of excellence but would not be considered "great." (Meyer suggests that many of Bach's *Inventions* exemplify this.) On the other hand some works seem to reach to heights of greatness but somehow do not quite "come off," in that they are not as strong in execution as they need to be. The best works are those which combine the highest order of excellence with the most profound expressive content. These are the landmarks of musical literature—the treasures of human culture. And while there never has been and no doubt never will be full agreement as to which pieces deserve the descriptions "excellent" or "great," enough agreement does exist about enough important music (music which might potentially have qualities of excellence and greatness) that examples of the "very good" are readily available for use in music education.

It would be unrealistic and unnecessary to aim for constant use of great music in teaching and learning, partly because of the obvious limitations of children's musical capacities and partly because people, of any age, should not be expected to operate at the farthest reaches of their abilities at all times. Some reasonableness of expectations is called for, in which music of a wide range of goodness is used, providing sufficient challenge for the particular age-group while at the same time providing musical enjoyment for immediate sharing. And occasionally it is helpful to use an "awful example"—a piece obviously deficient in excellence or expressiveness—as a way to make a particular point. To insist on studying nothing but the monuments of music literature, to rule out that large segment of music which, while well made and genuinely expressive is not of the *crème de la crème,* is to deprive a great many people of any musical satisfaction at all and to expect that all musical experience should be at the deepest level of involvement. This is certainly unnecessary. At the same time a heavy use of unimportant music, of "pretty" pieces with little muscle, of that vast realm of music which is not really bad but certainly is not very good, makes of music education a whipped-cream dessert, pleasant and light, but not to be considered an important part of educational fare. If the general level of musical quality is such that a constant movement toward the "better" is taking place; that is, a movement toward music of more refinement in structural excellence and more depth in expressive power, music education will be fulfilling its role reasonably and responsibly.

Two often-debated questions about suitable music for music education can be answered by applying the conceptions in the foregoing discussion. These are the questions of 1) the relevance or irrelevance of older music for modern experience, and 2) the propriety or impropriety of using popular music in music education. While both matters deserve more extended treatment than can be given here, a few comments should be made.

When a so-called work of art is weak in structure and superficial in expressiveness it is irrelevant to human experience *no matter when it was made*. Conversely, a work of excellence and genuine expressiveness, from any period in history, has the power to reveal a sense of feelingfulness to all who are capable of responding to it musically. The point of the previous discussion of the importance of using a wide variety of styles in music education is to insure that good music of any age can be perceived relevantly and responded to feelingfully. Of course much music of the past is "dated" and beside the point for modern sensibilities, but always and in every case such music is irrelevant because it is "of a time" and its time has passed. Many art works are limited by their dependence on fashion. They are not so much autonomous works, valuable in and of themselves, as they are instances of the peculiar mode of expression of their time. When the time has gone the value of the work is gone. Many such works can be regarded as "camp"—as old-fashioned, banal, "arty" in the worst sense, charming in their essential irrelevance.

The better the work of art the more it transcends its time of creation and is relevant to human experience in general. Of course styles change, but works of excellence and greatness are vital, living sources of insight into the human condition no matter how different in style from the one then current. The notion that art works should be regarded as "an expression of their time," (a popular idea in "Allied Arts" or "Humanities" approaches, about which some comments will be made in Chapter Ten), misses the point of art's value except for the most superficial works, which really *are* little more than "an expression of their time."

It is especially true of today's culture that good art of the past is readily accessible and widely acceptable. To concentrate on "the art of one's own time" to the exclusion of good art of *any* time is as provincial as the opposite; that is, insisting that only old art is good art. The criterion for choosing music, then, remains an essentially ahistorical òne —that sufficient excellence and expressiveness be present to widen the musical capabilities of the particular students being taught.

Does popular music qualify as a source of musical excellence and expressiveness? First, a distinction must be drawn between popular music and jazz, the latter being a musical style domain with a complex history, a well-developed literature, a rich variety and abundance of music of unquestionable excellence and profound expressiveness. While jazz still finds itself fighting the old, tired battle of its "impolite" origins, it is more and more being accepted for what it is—a fascinating and valuable source of musical experience.

But what of pop music? Here the question of musical value does have relevance, and, to complicate matters, the generation gap makes it difficult for communication to take place between music educators of varying ages and between teachers and students. As a result the debate about pop music in the schools often seems to have generated more heat than light. A few ideas from this chapter and previous ones might be of some help in thinking about this issue.

To "rule out of court" any music without regard to its inherent musical quality is to act from an irrelevant basis for judging musical value. Just because music is "pop music" does not, in and of itself, make it unsuitable for use in music education. The question to be asked about pop music is the same that should be asked about *any* music: is enough musical quality available here to help musical perception and reaction to grow? An answer to this question in regard to contemporary popular music must necessarily be based on personal and professional judgment. It can be argued—and well argued—that some popular music of the present time (an astonishing amount, as a matter of fact) is of extremely high quality in musical excellence and musical expressiveness. Much music of the Beatles, of Simon and Garfunkel, of many groups with unlikely—even bizarre—names and modes of dress, is 1) at least as good if not much better than the best popular music of any time in the past, and 2) of a musical level which transcends its pop context and becomes, in and of itself, musically valuable. To rule out such music from music education would be not only a loss of fine material, but, even worse, an artificial, aristocratic, snobbish mode of behavior, which can only make the music education enterprise seem artificial, aristocratic, snobbish.

At the same time it should be recognized that a vast wasteland of musical inanity exists in the pop music field. But, to be perfectly fair, this should not in any way be an indictment of pop music. Unlike music in which aesthetic value is the be-all and end-all, pop music does not primarily exist to serve aesthetic purposes. It exists primarily to serve social and psychological needs of teen-agers and this it does with great power and singular effectiveness. To say that most pop music is musically valueless is to say something which is certainly true, but is also beside the point. It is just as unfair to judge pop music as a whole by musical standards as it is to judge concert music by standards of social usefulness (does the opera last too long for keeping the after-concert dinner warm?, does it allow for enough intermissions to see what people are wearing?, etc.).

If music education is primarily aesthetic education it will include aesthetically valuable music of any sort. Music educators can recognize that some music serves other than aesthetic purposes and that non-aesthetic uses of music which are healthy, helpful to people, and not destructive of aesthetic sensitivity should be supported; perhaps not professionally but as parents, as citizens, as human beings concerned about other human needs in addition to aesthetic ones. Of course when non-aesthetic uses of music seem to be preventing people from growing musically the music educator must do all he can to resolve the conflict. This happens only rarely. Unfortunately, many music educators inadvertently *cause* a conflict between pop music and the development of musical sensitivity when they insist that pop music be compared with music of an aesthetic intent and force a choice between the two. This causes resentment, musical insecurity, and an inevitable erosion of confidence in the music educator as an understanding individual. Both for musical and personal reasons the differences in intent and value of pop music and art music should be recognized openly and accepted graciously. The benefits to children and to music education (not to mention the relief of reducing the number of arguments with teen-agers) should be considerable.

How can music education promote musical experiences of music and therefore help to share musical meaning more fully? Three major aspects of music education have evolved as the means by which musical learnings can take place: general music, performance, and music studied in company with its sister arts. The question must now be asked: How can each of these components of the program contribute to aesthetic education in music?

QUESTIONS FOR DISCUSSION

1. What advantages accrue from viewing all the arts from a "musical" base? What are some possible difficulties which might arise from doing so indiscriminately?

2. Give more examples of responses to music under each of the "non-musical" categories (excluding the "Technical-Critical"). What are some devices widely used to *promote* such non-musical responses? Do you agree that such practices should be called "non-music education"?

3. What are some dangers of regarding non-musical experiences as being proper for children—especially very young children? Can young children enjoy music musically? Can or should music education be primarily devoted to helping them do so?

4. The "Categories of Experiences of Music" apply, with some alterations, to experiences of every art. For each art (painting, dance, poetry, etc.) give examples of responses under each category. What does this imply for teaching all the arts aesthetically rather than non-aesthetically? Are there some leads to how the arts might be taught together and still be taught for the aesthetic value of each?

5. How do you feel about the issue of whether totally "sensuous" music can be regarded as "meaningful" or "musical" or "aesthetic"? How should you act about this issue as a practicing music educator?

6. Why it it so important that children be exposed to a wide variety of musical styles? What limitations are imposed by relying heavily on that music which they themselves can perform? Are the limitations even more severe when long periods of time are spent on music in a particularly "performable" style such as that using the pentatonic scale?

7. What practical aid for music education is supplied by the idea of judging music according to 1) excellence of construction and 2) power of expressiveness? How are such criteria valuable in avoiding "imposing one's own preferences" on other people?

8. Do you agree with the idea that popular music qualifies for use in music education if it is of high enough musical quality to be studied and experienced musically? Argue your case, especially as it applies to music education for teen-agers.

SUPPLEMENTARY READINGS

1. Langer, Susanne K., *Feeling and Form.* New York: Charles Scribner's Sons, 1953, Chapter 7, "The Image of Time," Chapter 8, "The Musical Matrix," Chapter 9, "The Living Work." (See comment under (2).)

2. Langer, Susanne K., *Philosophy in a New Key.* New York: Mentor Books,

1942, Chapter 8, "On Significance in Music." This chapter and the three listed in (1) contain Langer's most extended treatments of music. They will reward the patient reader with a great many valuable ideas about how music functions. If one chapter were to be selected, "The Living Work" in *Feeling and Form* would probably be the most immediately useful.

3. Meyer, Leonard B., *Emotion and Meaning in Music.* Chicago: The University of Chicago Press, 1956, Chapter 1, pp. 22–42, and the remainder of the book. After completing his discussion of the relation of affect and musical experience (pp. 22–42), Meyer presents detailed musical analyses employing Gestalt laws of pattern perception. While the serious student will want to study this material carefully, a quicker reading will serve to introduce the principles upon which Meyer builds his theory of musical expectation.

4. Meyer, Leonard B., *Music, the Arts, and Ideas.* Chicago: The University of Chicago Press, 1967. Part I contains five previously published articles on music and art, of which Chapters 1, 2 and 3 are extremely helpful discussions of various aspects of music. Chapter 5, "The End of the Renaissance?," is a most provocative treatment of randomness in art. The remainder of the book presents as lucid a discussion of contemporary artistic trends, especially of "total serialism" in music, as one is likely to find in the tortuous literature on this subject.

5. Reimer, Bennett, "Information Theory and the Analysis of Musical Meaning," *Council for Research in Music Education,* Bulletin No. 2, Winter, 1964. A discussion of the uses and limitations of information theory and analysis in general for developing musical perceptivity.

6. Valentine, C. W., *The Experimental Psychology of Beauty.* London: Methuen & Co. Ltd., 1962 (published in the U.S.A. by Dover Publications, Inc., New York), Chapter XII, "Music and the Expression of Emotions or 'Meaning.'" This interesting book reports on a wide range of experimental studies in the arts. Chapter XII is especially pertinent to music education. Chapters X and XI also deal with music. Aesthetic educators will find valuable material throughout the book.

CHAPTER EIGHT

music education as aesthetic education: the general music program

As one looks back over the history of general music through its many phases and its many names one begins to feel that more words have been spilled on this subject than any other, save, perhaps, sex and the Civil War. There is probably no older, no deeper, no more abiding problem in all of music education than the problem of music in general education, which is why it always has been and no doubt always will be a topic of great timeliness and of great urgency. Much as one might hesitate to add even more words to the many now existing, new conditions call for a rethinking of old problems. The problem of general music will not be "solved"—it will only be dealt with differently as new viewpoints arise, as new goals become acceptable, as new beliefs become current. The obligation of music education is to insure that the general music program mirrors the best thought of the profession as its thinking evolves.

This chapter can do little more than to sketch the broad outlines of the general music program in the shape of our philosophy of music education. To deal with all the particulars would of course be impossible in the present context, but the direction those particulars need to take can be shown. The implementation of the program in the direction of aesthetic education should occupy the efforts of many music educators for many years to come.

Before beginning the discussion proper, however, a preliminary question should be asked. A central tenet of the philosophy presented here has been that music education should be primarily aesthetic education. The question is, must the general music program *always* be aesthetic education?

American schools typically expect the general music program to serve various functions in addition to the teaching and learning of music. Reflecting the variety of uses of music in society, various non-aesthetic activities of the school employ music as a utilitarian component. School ceremonies, festivals, athletic events, meetings, etc. call for music as a pleasant diversion, as a rallying point for school spirit, as an aid in getting children down the auditorium aisles and into their seats with a minimum of fuss, as a time-filler between acts of the school play, etc. Often the general music teacher is expected to provide the leadership for these functions and the students are expected to have learned how to behave in appropriate ways.

None of this is essentially aesthetic in purpose, music being used as a means toward non-musical ends. And none of it really requires the services of a highly-trained music educator. Most if not all of these uses of music could be handled quite well by a good amateur song leader-piano thumper-crowd organizer, of which there are many among school-teachers and parents. One of the major reasons for the comparatively low status of general music teachers is the feeling, usually subconscious but real nevertheless, that much of what such teachers do could be done as well by others of lesser training. Very little can be done to counteract this situation, either by general music teachers or their professional organization, so long as arguments are directed toward the essentially non-musical aspects of general music and justifications are based on those aspects.

To be an effective aesthetic educator in music requires, as this book, it is hoped, has made clear, aesthetic and pedagogical insight and expertise far beyond the casual, amateur-musician level. Further, the business of the music educator as aesthetic educator is of an importance worlds removed from the utilitarian values of music. When the general music teacher regards himself as an aesthetic educator, when the music education profession regards him as such, when schools are educated to the idea of aesthetic education as the primary purpose of the general music program, it becomes impossible to regard the enterprise and the teachers responsible for it with anything less than the highest seriousness and the highest regard. For what is being dealt with in aesthetic education are among the highest values of society—the values of artistic significance and the significance of human experience.

So both on the side of teaching and the side of learning general music should be, essentially, aesthetic education. At the same time, the non-aesthetic uses of music are perfectly valid and quite necessary to society. The music teacher must recognize that, as with practically every other subject taught in school, some obligations exist at the periphery of the subject. If accepted with graciousness, good humor, an attitude of "these are some of the things that go along with my job and should be done effectively, even if they are not the most important things I do," the children, the school and society can then accept them similarly. The general music program can be openly and avowedly an aesthetic education program with attention to other matters as required. In all dealings with policy-making groups the general music teacher should promote that view, basing his position on what is of primary importance about his subject but not neglecting or denigrating the auxiliary uses of music. The quality of his argument for music education as aesthetic education will determine whether he and his subject are accepted as an important part of the educational enterprise. The philosophy offered here has been devoted to that argument.

Music education has a dual obligation to society. The first is to develop the talents of those who are gifted musically, for their own personal benefit, for the benefit of the society which will be served by them, for the benefit of the art of music which depends on a continuing supply of composers, performers, conductors, scholars, teachers. The second obligation is to develop the aesthetic sensitivity to music of all people regardless of their individual levels of musical talent, for their own personal benefit, for the benefit of society which needs an active cultural life, for the benefit of the art of music which depends on a continuing supply of sympathetic, sensitive consumers. These two obligations are mutually supportive: the neglect of either one inevitably weakens both.

Some needs of the musically talented are in excess of the needs of the general population and must be fulfilled through special education—special in the sense of serving a relatively small proportion of the population. Other musical needs are common to all people and must be fulfilled for everyone. It has been customary in music education to regard the performance program as special education for the talented and the general music program as general education for the untalented. This has had the unfortunate effect of weakening both parts of the program. The performance program suffers from an intolerable level of irrelevance while the general music program suffers from an intolerable level of superficiality. These weaknesses are not likely to be overcome so long as these two major aspects of the music program are viewed as serving two separate groups of people. The suggestion made here is that both the performance program and the general music program be regarded as serving the aesthetic needs of all students regardless of talent, with each program serving special musical needs as an important addition to its offerings. The next chapter will focus on the performance program as aesthetic education for students of all levels of talent, while the present chapter deals with the general music program for precisely the same students; that is, *all* students.

When an individual student's level of musical talent seems to be such that special training is in order the philosophical problem of what he should be taught has largely been solved. Technical problems arise: Who would be a good private teacher?, How much public performance should be arranged for?, How can a richer than usual musical environment be provided?, etc. But the question of what to do in the first place has fairly clear answers. Quite the reverse is true when the problem is one of choosing, from all possible things one might study about music and all possible modes of studying it, that which is most appropriate for all students. Given the varying capacities of people, given the limitations of time available for study, given a wide range of interest and desire, how can one share what is most valuable about one's subject with most people in the most effective way? This is the central question of general education—general education in *any* subject.

The curriculum reform revolution in American education has been devoted to answering this question in ways relevant to the times in which we live and the foreseeable future. While the problem of general education is an everpresent one, calling for new answers as conditions change, the present time has been one of unusual activity in this regard, no doubt because a previous neglect of the problem made the need for change very great. The most typical answer to the question of general education in our times has been, simply put, that the most important content of every subject is that subject's "structure"—its core of interrelated conceptions and modes of behavior which make it a unified, distinguishable discipline.[1] Education can share this "heart of the matter" about each subject by focusing major effort on teaching it to all children at every stage of their development, in ways relevant to both the subject's

---

[1] The most influential and easily understood explanation of this idea is Jerome Bruner, *The Process of Education* (New York: Vintage Books, 1960), especially Chapter 2.

own nature and to the children's evolving modes of understanding. Curriculum development has consisted of an effort to put these general principles into practice.

This book has tried to explain the nature of the arts and the art of music according to the most widely accepted aesthetic point of view of our times. The "structure" of music, it has been suggested, is the created sound-complex of tendencies and inhibitions which are expressive of the conditions of subjective reality. In this particular subject—the art of music—"teaching for structure" consists of developing the powers of perception of tendency-inhibition sound-complexes, in contexts which encourage feelingful reactions to the expressive conditions they present. The combination of musical perception and musical reaction is musical aesthetic experience, this being the peculiar mode of "understanding" or of "knowing" in the field of the arts. General education in music, then, consists primarily of developing the abilities of every child to have aesthetic experiences of music, using strategies appropriate to the child's changing capacities for perception and reaction. The "heart of the matter" in music is the expressiveness of sound, and the "heart of the matter" in music education is to help every child experience the expressiveness of sound as fully as he is capable of doing so.

The principles for aesthetic education in music stated in previous chapters are the broad guidelines for insuring that general music education will be relevant both to music and to people. The first of these is perhaps the most basic—that the primary material for study at every stage of development be good music. The word "good," as should be clear at this point, does not refer to any particular type, style or medium of music, but to qualities of excellent construction and genuine expressiveness. These qualities are found in music of all types and all levels of complexity. While no infallible yardstick exists for identifying good music the combined experience of many musicians and educators has made available a large body of literature of good quality and usefulness.

To search for good new music from every possible source that culture contains is a continuing obligation of music education. It is of particular importance at the present time because of the need, which music education shares with practically every other subject, of bringing the material studied in school closer into line with the subject as it exists outside of school. Whenever new music is added to the "tried and true," as it must be if music education is to take advantage of the rich diversity of good music available to it, risks are run that poor music will creep into use along with music of high quality. This risk is inevitable. One important safeguard against wasting precious time and weakening musical taste by using trite, artificial music, is the inherent musical sensitivity of the teacher. There is no substitute, when all is said and done, for a general music teacher who is a specialist in general music for a particular age group, who possesses a high order of musical training, aesthetic sensitivity, and pedagogical expertise, and who is devoted to sharing the enjoyment of the art of music with all children. Aesthetic education calls for no less than teachers of such caliber, for good aesthetic education is without any question among the most difficult kinds of education to achieve. As aesthetic education in music becomes more pervasive the necessity for specialist teachers will no doubt become more obvious.

The delicate task of choosing good music is made more difficult by the necessity of using music sufficiently accessible to be aesthetically experienced while at the same time sufficiently challenging to stretch the powers of musical perception and reaction. As a general rule children should experience some music which can be fully grasped or close to it, some which is far beyond their powers of understanding but gives inklings of the riches which are available, and a great deal of music which is aesthetically satisfying but complex enough to warrant continuing study over a long period of time. A sort of normal curve of accessibility is in operation, the ends of the curve representing the very easy and the very difficult, the center representing the bulk of material which is somewhere in between. As children mature musically the music moves from the difficult end of the curve into the center, as pieces at the easy end are dropped off and new ones are added at the difficult end. At every grade level the curve should be of generally the same shape, insuring a reasonable balance of accessibility. When the curve becomes skewed toward the very easy or the very complex the program inevitably becomes superficial or academic. Students with varying levels of musical perception should find, within the normal curve, enough material which serves their particular needs for immediate gratification, partial gratification with partial challenge, and great challenge with glimpses of future gratification. The highly talented will tend to operate toward one end of the curve and those with limited musical capacities at the other. For all children a wide diversity of aesthetic pleasure will be available within the spectrum of music used.

The general music teacher is the person who must control the shape of musical content for each child and each class of children, for no one else is as well acquainted with their musical needs and capacities. As in the matter of musical quality, decisions about musical complexity are of a subtlety requiring nothing less than a highly trained, sensitive, devoted specialist—not only who is a specialist in music, but who also specializes in general music for a particular age group; elementary, junior high school or senior high school. To think that many teachers can be successful at all levels is to underestimate the delicacy of the task.

The use of good music of reasonable complexity is a necessary but not sufficient condition for an effective general music program. The manner in which the music is treated is crucial to success. It has been suggested often in this book that the general mode of musical study is one which follows the pattern of 1) musical experience, 2) musical study, 3) musical re-experience.[2] This pattern puts the actual experience of music where it belongs—first and last. Musical study is conceived not as an end but always as a means to the end which really matters—the deeper experience of music.

Isolating the study of music from musical experience insures a sterility which can only weaken aesthetic sensitivity. But it would be a grave error to assume that musical sensitivity will increase without serious study. Again, a delicate state of balance must exist, in which components of experience and study are manipulated to provide the best "mix" for each student and each class. As a general rule the "experience-study-experience" pattern will get larger in scope as children grow older. In the primary grades, for example, one would not usually expect an entire period to be spent on uninterrupted listening or composing, or a period to be spent on uninterrupted analyzing or rehearsing. This might well be possible at the high school level, where a class could, for example, listen to a work for an entire period, explore various aspects of its structure in several succeeding periods, and listen to the whole piece again several days after the first complete hearing, the whole unit being experienced as coherent. For young children a rapid alternation of experiencing, studying and re-experiencing is necessary, commensurate with their more limited powers of concentration and conceptualization. It is likely that a 30-minute period in second grade, for example, will contain many small patterns of singing-exploring the song-singing it again; listening-exploring the piece-listening again; etc. And of course the "a-b-a" pattern will not be followed slavishly, a string of "a's" or "b's" being perfectly useful for various purposes or a "b-a-b" pattern being used for a particular reason. The skillful teacher will use strategies which provide for plenty of change of pace, which are appropriate for the age level, which give the children a sense of unity so they know what they are doing and why they are doing it, and most important, which make perfectly obvious to

---

[2] This is an idea of long standing in music education. Compare, for example, James L. Mursell and Mabelle Glenn, *The Psychology of School Music Teaching* (Morristown, N.J., Silver Burdett Co., 1931), Chapter 3, "Musical Learning."

the children that musical experience is the end and study the means, rather than the reverse.

For the "study" part of musical learning a teacher is needed who, first, is sophisticated about the workings of music and, second, is skillful in clarifying musical content in a wide variety of ways relevant to the particular children being taught. Weakness in either aspect—musicianship or teaching ability—will seriously affect the quality of instruction. Since musical expressiveness is a function of identifiable musical processes it is essential that the teacher—at *every* level of music education—be skilled in revealing the conditions of musical affect to all children. The general music teacher is a specialist in teaching about melody, rhythm, harmony, tone color, texture, form, style, through particular pieces of music but in ways which show how these elements operate in all music. The skills required for doing this successfully are as complex as any in education.

How can musical content be studied effectively? Several approaches have been used in music education with varying degrees of success. The most pervasive way to study music in the general music program, from kindergarten through eighth grade, has traditionally been through singing. So strong are the ties to a singing approach, both historically and in amount of time spent as compared with other modes of musical instruction, that general music is often called "vocal music." It is inconceivable to many music educators that there could be or should be any difference between a vocal music program and anything which might be called "general music." This attitude is reflected not only in school practices but in teacher education, in which a "vocal-general" curriculum, or something like it, is the most common course for future general music teachers.

Several limitations of singing argue against reliance on it as the sole or major means for studying or experiencing music. The songs children can sing are inevitably of limited complexity compared with their powers of musical perception and reaction. The gap between the ability to sing and the ability to experience music musically grows wider as children grow older, until in upper elementary and junior high school grades the disparity has usually become painful for both students and teachers. No amount of searching for songs which "appeal," which are "psychologically acceptable," which are "masculine" for the boys or "touching" for the girls, will make up for the fact that a diet of songs is inadequate for the increasingly sophisticated musical needs of children. This is especially true if the general music program, from the very start, has helped children come to grips with many kinds of music of a wide diversity of musical complexity. With an ever-broadening acquaintance with the riches available in the realm of music the likelihood that song-singing alone will satisfy aesthetic needs is, and should be, small.

This is not to suggest that singing is irrelevant or unimportant. As the most accessible means of music making, singing will always be of great usefulness as a tool for making many conceptions about musical expressiveness tangible through direct manipulation. Also, singing in and of itself offers musical and aesthetic rewards which should be reaped by many children. However, the benefits of singing as an activity in and of itself are properly cultivated by the performance program. In general music, singing is a means to aesthetic ends; useful, necessary, pleasurable, but not sufficient. To the extent that singing remains as over-emphasized as it sometimes is at present the musical learnings of many children will, of necessity, be limited to those which are song-connected and singing-connected. Important as these are they represent only a fraction of the potentially fruitful learnings children can enjoy. An effective aesthetic education program in general music will use singing as one of many ways to help musical sensitivity grow.

The comments about singing apply equally to the playing of instruments as a part of general music, although the built-in difficulties of instrumental performance have naturally limited its use as compared with singing. The playing of instruments of all kinds can be a most effective tool for increasing the sensitivity of children to the riches of musical expressiveness and will be employed by the general music teacher at all levels. As with singing, playing serves the purposes of aesthetic education when it helps clarify, through direct experience, the expressive nature of music. It can do so, as can singing, in a great many ways, and is therefore a necessary component of general musical study. But again, as with singing, the special benefits of instrumental study as a field of its own are the proper domain of the performance program.

Composition is a mode of musical study which can be most effective for clarifying how music works and for giving the actual experience of bringing music to birth. At every age children can and should be given many opportunities both to explore the inner workings of music through composition and to use what they are learning about music in self-created pieces. Notational skills can be cultivated through composition quite effectively and can then be used to advantage in all aspects of general music. The sense of personal musical responsibility which composition gives is most healthy in bringing musical processes into intimate contact with the child's experience. The question is highly debatable as to whether their own composing gives children an understanding of what actually transpires in the act of creation of an artist composer. This is true as well about whether singing or playing gives children an understanding of what the artist performer experiences.[3] But it is certainly true that involvement in music making—composing and performing—is an effective component of musical study for helping aesthetic perception and reaction to become more sensitive, more discerning, more subtle, more penetrating. Every child deserves the opportunity to work personally and originally with musical materials to the fullest extent of his abilities. In the process of composing and performing as means to aesthetic education unusual talents will inevitably come to light and these should be cultivated as fully as possible. All children can become more musically responsive through music making, which therefore constitutes an important element of general music education.

But necessary as performing and composing might be they do not by themselves provide as much opportunity to share the insights available in music as children can and should share. Musical experience for all people at all ages is the same in its basic conditions: perceiving and reacting to the expressiveness of sound. This experience is of course an integral part of performing and composing but is not dependent on either. The glorious thing about music and the other arts, which makes them accessible to all people, is that one can share their significance whether or not one has the ability to engage in their production. And no matter how much ability in production a person might have, his ability to enjoy art will always outstrip his own ability to produce. It would be a tragic limitation of musical experience to confine it to the level of any person's ability to perform or compose. The general music program should help children develop their capacities for musical experience in ways which are not encumbered by constant reliance on production. The development of musical listening ability is a basic obligation of general music as aesthetic education.

Listening has suffered from such severe mishandling in music education and as a result has had such a "bad press" for so long that the notion of regarding it as a major activity in its own right will inevitably suggest a general music program rife with the weaknesses which plague "listening" in much present music teaching. One immediately has visions of a lecturing teacher, a class either bored to the point of stupor or rowdy to the point of riot, an interminably revolving record scratching out unlistened-to sounds, a feeling of desperation on the part of the teacher that this great music is producing an absolute zero in the way of

---

3 For some insightful comments about this matter see Foster McMurray, "Pragmatism in Music Education," in Nelson B. Henry, ed., *Basic Concepts in Music Education* (Chicago: National Society for the Study of Education, 1958, Part I), pp. 44–47.

response, a feeling of bewilderment on the part of the children that any of those indiscriminate sounds are to be taken seriously. Given the vast, bleak wasteland of much which passes for "listening activity," it is certainly understandable that many teachers have either abandoned its use in favor of production activities, which at the least keep children busy, or listen to only such "music" which is so non-musical that short doses are bound to produce something resembling curiosity, and therefore enough life to reassure the teacher that he does not have thirty-three cases of catalepsy on his hands.

It is of the first order of importance that the resources of the music education profession and allied fields be brought to bear on the development of materials which teach listening skills in interesting, effective, musically valid ways. That this is possible of achievement there is no doubt. If even a fraction of the effort which goes into materials for production activities could be channeled into the development of clever but honest listening materials a dramatic change for the better would occur. There are signs at present that this is happening, although, unfortunately, new technological capabilities have produced some listening devices which are gimmicky, non-musical and non-educative. What is needed are ways to help children perceive what is actually expressive in music they are listening to, so that the power of the music can be felt. No amount of non-musical picturizations, moving or still, of color wheels or amusing drawings or charming narrations will fill the bill. Listening aids should focus on musically expressive events and characteristics using simple, descriptive, non-emotional and non-interpretive terms. The conceptions about melody, harmony, rhythm, etc. being built through singing, playing, composing, notating, bodily movements, discussing, reading, etc. should find fruition in listening, as they come to life and take on aesthetic significance through actually experiencing them in important music.

Listening is the essential mode of musical experiencing. Some people will achieve musical listening experience as they perform or compose, but *all* people will share the art of music directly through its peculiar sense modality—listening. To call listening "merely listening," as is so often done, is to call musical experience "merely musical experience." The word "merely" is a recognition of the passivity and irrelevance of typical listening methodologies. But the cultivation of musical listening abilities so that musical experience can be what it should be—intensely involved, perceptive, feelingful, creative, richly significant and satisfying—is the central challenge and contribution of general music as aesthetic education.

To meet this challenge it is necessary for musical study to include a large element of conscious, careful exploration of the inner workings of music. In the "study" part of music education a single, fundamental purpose should be served—to bring more clearly to perception the expressive conditions being presented by the sounds of music. Whether listening, singing, playing, composing, music reading, etc., the process of exploration is the major way to study music so that musical experience itself can become deeper.

The following words are suggestive of the many ways that musical exploration can take place: show, discuss, manipulate, imitate, compare, describe, define, identify, classify, modify, rearrange, reshape, vary, combine, contrast, develop, inspect, observe, amplify, reconstruct, characterize, infer, disclose, clarify, demonstrate, explain, appraise, discern, recall, locate, invent. All these shadings of exploration and many more one could add to the list can be described as the process of "analyzing." Analysis should not be thought of as the dry, sterile picking apart of the bare bones of music. Certainly it can be this and often is, especially in college music theory classes. Such "analysis" would be the death of aesthetic education. When analysis is conceived as an active, involved exploration of the living qualities of music, and when analysis is in constant and immediate touch with musical experience itself, it is the essential means for making musical enjoyment more obtainable.

Analysis requires tools. In order to "show, discuss, manipulate," etc., a set of signs—a language—is needed which conceptualizes the expressive conditions of sound so that these conditions can be "shown, discussed, manipulated," etc. The more conditions of expressiveness which can be conceptualized the more abundantly can musical expressiveness be analyzed (explored). As has been suggested in many places throughout this book the language of musical conceptions should be descriptive of musical conditions; not interpretive of those conditions, for it is the *conditions themselves* which should cause feeling and not the teacher's interpretation of them. For the musical element of rhythm, for example, helpful conceptions include tempo (fast, slow, getting faster, getting slower), pulse (regular, irregular, strong, weak, grouping into meter), accent, length of notes, rhythmic patterns, etc. Some of the conceptions in melody are intervals, length, direction, shape, register, structure. In harmony conceptions of expressive conditions include consonance, dissonance, density, tonality, atonality, cadences, modulations, shape, prominence, etc. For form conceptions include repetition, variation, contrast, development, binary, ternary, free form, etc. To the extent that such conceptions are 1) true to music, 2) treated in imaginative ways, 3) kept in intimate and constant contact with actual music actually experienced, 4) consistent from grade to grade so they can deepen over a long period of time, 5) explored at musical levels of difficulty compatible with the children's abilities at various stages of development, they will be among the most useful tools in music education.

The general music program as a whole will include a wide diversity of activities relevant to musical experience revolving around the major goal of instruction: increasing aesthetic sensitivity to music. Neither an "activities-only" approach nor a "listening-only" approach will be sufficient, nor will an unstructured, unrelated conglomeration of listenings plus activities. Each must reinforce the other in consistent, planned, ever-widening circles of musical perception and reaction. A diagram of such a program might look like the one on page 123.

At the center of the general music program is the be-all and end-all of music education—the development of musical sensitivity. All activities and all combinations of activities point in the direction of improving musical perception and reaction, giving the program its thrust, its cohesiveness, its reason for being. This central goal, which provides the organizing structure for all particular activities, has been absent from too many traditional general music programs, with the result that such programs have been empty in purpose, loose in structure, weak in impact. General music need not suffer from these traditional ills. It should not if it becomes aesthetic education.

The circle representing first grade is very close to musical experience itself, signifying the necessity, when teaching very young children, to keep all study in intimate contact with music as immediately experienced. Musical study should be of relatively short duration, never separated from concrete application, always taking its point of departure from music as felt. As the child grows older the circles widen, indicating increasing ability to study for longer periods of time, to conceptualize more subtly, to grasp more complex relations among the many elements of music, to understand the relevance of more complex activities. From grades 1–6 this process is very gradual and of the same general nature. Each of the activities—listening, singing, playing, etc.—is present at every grade level at progressively more challenging levels of complexity.

At around the seventh grade level a distinct change takes place in children and therefore in education. This is the age when for most children in American society mental abilities begin to shift from childish modes to adult modes. The child moves from the stage of "concrete operations," in which concepts, in order to have meaning, must be closely related to concrete experience, to the stage of "formal operations," in which the ability to think in terms of systems of conceptions begins its

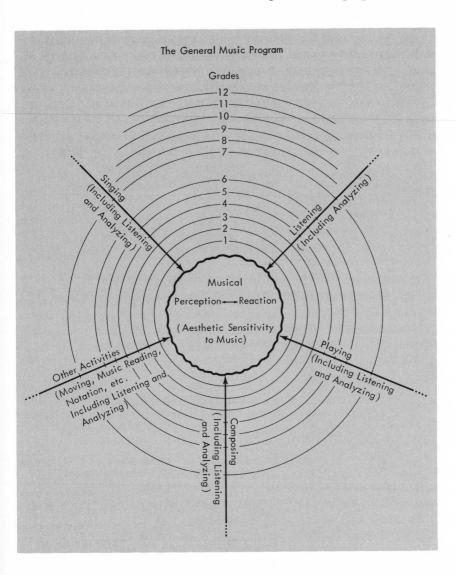

The General Music Program

Grades

growth toward adult modes of mentality.[4] Education must reflect this developmental change by approaching things from a shifted base of assumptions and expectations. This does not mean that beginning with junior high school one can treat children as if they were miniature gradu-

---

[4] For a discussion of Jean Piaget's conception of mental growth and its implications for education, see Bruner, *The Process of Education,* Chapter 3.

ate students. To take the change in mental abilities as an excuse to abandon musical involvement in favor of "academic study" would be tragic, for music education should never, at any stage of growth, abandon what it exists to serve—musical experience itself. However one can begin to expect a larger view, a more subtle understanding, a broader approach, consistent with the early teen-age youngster's increasingly adult modes of thought.

Because the more mature nature of the teen-ager's mental processes have not been generally recognized in music education the content of the general music program at the junior high level has often suffered from childishness, making it particularly difficult to teach successfully. It is to be hoped that as new and more acceptable materials are developed this problem will fade. In the diagram of the general music program given here the seventh grade begins the sequence of secondary general music, as distinct from elementary general music in grades 1–6. As children move through the teen-age years the disparity between the ability to produce through singing, playing, composing, and the ability to experience music sophisticatedly through listening, analyzing, discussing, evaluating, becomes so wide as to be intolerable for many people. The general music program, therefore, gradually diminishes its reliance on production activities and strengthens the content of listening and listening-related activities. At the same time the performance program increases its offerings to serve the needs of all children who want to produce music, including those who are particularly talented in performance. At the high school level a variety of music courses should be offered ranging from general music, which continues the basic study of musical expressiveness in all its aspects, through various history and literature courses and more detailed music theory and composition courses including, in both history and theory, courses to meet the needs of children particularly talented in those areas. Also included should be the opportunity to study music in the context of the wider domain of the arts. Chapter Ten will focus on this particular aspect of the program.

Although musical sensitivity should grow from grade to grade every grade by itself should provide the richest, most totally musical environment possible for the children of that grade. The best preparation for more enjoyable musical experience in the future is the most enjoyable musical experience that is possible in the present. A general music program so future-oriented that satisfying musical experiences are constantly "somewhere up ahead" can only deprive children of one of life's major pleasures, not only in their lives as it is being lived but for their future as well. Aesthetic significance is a deepening of immediate experience. The general music program is the means of providing aesthetic depth to the musical experience of all children at every point in their school-time years. It would be difficult to imagine a more humanising contribution to the quality of every child's life.

QUESTIONS FOR DISCUSSION

1. Why has the problem of music in general education been such a long lasting one? Is it likely that a final solution will be found some day?

2. What difficulties have been raised for the status of general music by trying to justify itself on the basis of its non-aesthetic contributions? Should these contributions be totally halted?

3. Do you agree that the general music program has tended to suffer from a high level of superficiality? What forces outside music education itself promote a certain superficiality? Are there any forces outside the profession which would strongly support more substance in the general music program?

4. Try to restate the explanation of what "teaching for structure" means in music, using more technical, musical terms. What would counterpart explanations sound like in 1) other arts, 2) non-art subjects?

5. Do you agree that if music education becomes more sophisticated as aesthetic education, specialist teachers are likely to be needed more than at present? What problems would this present if it were true?

6. What are some practical outgrowths of the suggestion that music studied should range from easy to difficult in a sort of "normal curve" of accessibility? Are present general music materials helpful in reaching such a goal?

7. Give examples of actual teaching strategies which would follow the general outline of "experience-study-experience." How can these strategies be adapted to different age levels?

8. What balance of singing, listening, composing, playing, notating, conceptualizing, moving, would you think would be most effective at primary, intermediate, junior high, senior high levels? What practices would insure that all these activities are aiming toward deeper musical sensitivity?

9. If the general music program is to be more consistently musical, should some change in the education of general music teachers be made? What might some changes consist of?

CHAPTER NINE

music education as aesthetic education: the performance program

For many music educators and for a large portion of the general public the terms "music education" and "performance" are synonymous. During much of this century the educational and social climates in America have been most favorable to the kind of group activity fostered by performing organizations. With the attractiveness of such groups, their wholesomeness for children and enjoyable contributions to cultural life, the tangibility with which they demonstrate results of effort, their ability to inspire the loyalty of children and parents, the performance program has achieved a size and a complexity unmatched in all the world. Although musical results reflect the wide diversity of circumstances under which American education operates, a good many schools have produced organizations of astonishingly high performance standards. Surely the field of music education, and particularly those responsible for performance activities, have good reason to be proud of their unique contribution to society.

But just as every other part of the school curriculum has come under scrutiny in recent years, the performance program finds itself being examined according to changing conditions of education. Both from within and without the music education profession come new questions, new concerns, new expectations. Old arguments stressing the value of performance no longer seem to make much impression, and new arguments, reflecting altered conceptions of what constitutes high quality education, have not yet had time to be fully articulated. The need for serious thought about the function of performance in music education is most pressing.

This would not be the case if performance could continue to be regarded as either 1) special education for the musically talented or 2) an extra-curricular "activity" program on the level of special-interest clubs, social groups, etc. Neither of these alternatives is acceptable. On the one hand a great many children involved in performance are not unusually talented and most have no intention of pursuing music professionally. On the other hand there are values in performance which place it in a completely different category from extra-curricular "activities." The music education profession, recognizing this, has fought long and hard—with a high degree of success—for acceptance of performance as a member in good standing of the school's regular curriculum. But if performance is not to be regarded as special education and if it is not to be regarded as an educational frill how does it justify its existence as a bona fide curricular offering? This is precisely the question which has not been satisfactorily answered and which must be answered if the performance program is to be supported as it deserves.

The answer offered in this book is that performance is an essential component of music education as aesthetic education. This places performance in the strong position of being relevant for all children rather than just the talented few, and of contributing in its unique way to the central goal of music education rather than to the fringe benefits of music education. If it can be established that the performance program can in fact be so regarded the weaknesses of specialism and peripheralism will have been overcome for once and for all. And until these weaknesses are overcome performance must continue to be on the defensive, trying to justify itself on the basis of outmoded educational values. Fortunately for performance and fortunately for music education arguments do exist which have the potential to overcome the weaknesses which have plagued the performance program throughout its history. In the context of education today and in the foreseeable future these weaknesses have become more than just troublesome—they have become intolerable. This chapter —or this book—cannot at one stroke solve the entire problem of justifying performance. But it can indicate how the problem can be approached and what needs to be done by the profession to implement its solution.

Before beginning the discussion of performance as aesthetic education, however, the same preliminary question asked about the general music program must be asked about the performance program. That is, must the performance program *always* be aesthetic education?

The two traditionally recognized contributions of performance—that it develops musical talent and that it serves many social needs—are rooted in facts of American life. Neither contribution can serve to justify the existence of performance as a full-fledged curricular subject but each has values which should be recognized and supported as adjuncts to the main educational purpose of performance.

The identification, encouragement, and development of talented performers remains an essential role of music education. It would be a great loss to many individuals, to the art of music, to society as a whole, if music education were to abdicate this role or dilute it. Any resistance on the part of performance teachers to the notion of performance as aesthetic education is likely to be based on the assumption that aesthetic education implies a weakening of the performance program in its ability to serve the talented. If this were so resistance would be justified. But precisely the opposite should happen if good music education is the goal of performance. The needs of the talented should be better served rather than worse, while at the same time the musical needs of all children are being met. The performance program can and must provide a context in which children can fulfill as much of their potential as performers as is possible. By itself the development of high levels of talent does not constitute music education as aesthetic education. But to think that aesthetic education in music ignores the musically talented is to misconstrue its nature. Music education as aesthetic education is inclusive of music education as talent education.

In the matter of serving non-musical needs the performance program is in the same position as the general music program, although, unfortunately, much more stock has been placed on the value of such service by performance than by general music. This fact has become a source of embarrassment to the profession, as slick techniques of salesmanship continue to be employed by portions of the performance "establishment" at the same time that music education struggles to become educationally respectable. In the recent past both the professional literature and the commercial literature of the field of music education were heavily laden with non-musical justifications for school music. The performance program especially was "sold" rather than "justified." And while a good deal of success was achieved in "selling" performance to the public the educational market has changed so radically in recent years that the old methods of salesmanship have become not only ineffective but debilitating as well. As in *Death of a Salesman,* the continued use of old techniques in a changed market can only lead to alienation and dissolution. Performance can no longer sell itself on the basis of its contribution to social skills or physical health or moral behavior or citizenship training or the need for rewards such as uniforms, medals, "A" ratings, and the like. If such unsupportable and irrelevant claims are all that performance has to offer then performance.is in deep trouble. At a time when every subject must demonstrate that it can make important contributions to the quality of children's lives, justifications for a large, expensive, time and energy-consuming performance program had better be at a high level of educational respectability. That such justifications for performance do in fact exist makes it even more unfortunate to continue to rely on specious arguments.

Recognizing that the educational world is rapidly outgrowing the old rationales for performance the professional literature has begun to exhibit anxiety symptoms about some of the more obviously non-aesthetic functions of the performance program. The marching band has come under heavy fire, as have contests, too many programs which are almost entirely at the level of non-musical entertainment, etc. The concern with such activities is that they are not germane to music education as a serious field of study, and to represent music eduction as consisting primarily of such activities is to prevent the profession from being regarded as an important member of the educational community.

But while it is true that activities which interfere with music education as aesthetic education can weaken the profession, it must be remembered that, as with the general music program, American society expects certain non-musical functions to be served by the performance program. Rather than beating its breast over this situation the music education profession would do well to accept it graciously and patiently. It is unnecessary for music education to refuse to serve some social needs which happen to be music-related. It is disastrous, however, to try to justify music education by its service to such needs. The more clearly the performance program can articulate its value as aesthetic education, the more solidly it supports its role as musical education, the more seriously it takes its obligations to increase the aesthetic sensitivity of its students, the less troublesome or burdensome or embarrassing will its non-aesthetic functions be. A performance program which is essentially musical, which justifies itself accordingly, which expends its major efforts on its essential purpose, can afford to give a reasonable amount of peripheral service without endangering its status. The risk of superficiality comes not from the existence of some fringe benefits but from not having a convincing, solid educational role to which the fringe benefits are attached.

What unique contributions to aesthetic education can the performance program make? Many people would answer this question by asserting that performing activities by their very nature must have a positive effect on aesthetic sensitivity. That children are actively engaged in performing music and are progressing in their ability to perform is often taken as clear evidence that their understanding, their sensitivity, their preferences, their attitudes, are all progressing in the direction of a deeper grasp of music and a heightened appreciation of its aesthetic values. In fact, many people take the position, consciously or unconsciously, that a child's level of musical sensitivity is *equivalent* to his level of performing ability, and in order to raise the former one must raise the latter.

Unfortunately for the children engaged in performance, unfortunately for the performance program and for music education, and unfortunately for the general level of musical sensitivity of American culture, the evidence on effects of performance experience in the schools does not seem to bear out the assumption about its aesthetic efficacy. Research tends to indicate that there is little if any relation between school performance activities and subsequent tastes or preferences for music. Even involvement in music making activities after high school graduation seems to be only minimally related to the level of involvement while in school.[1] One cannot look to presently existing research studies for final answers about the relation of performance to musical sensitivity, but one can also not ignore the existing indications that this relationship is equivocal.

At the level of everyday experience one also finds an uncertain relationship between the level of activity of performance programs and the musical sensitivity of the children involved in them. Many music educators, including performance directors, suspect that many if not most children seem to have been untouched in basic aesthetic understandings by their activities as performers. Certainly some children seem to be profoundly affected, as evidenced by those who go into music professionally. But they represent a very small portion of the involved population and even their general level of musical understanding is often found to be shockingly low by the college teachers who become responsible for their professional training. Difficult as it may be to acknowledge, the notion that performance automatically has positive effects on musical sensitivity is far from convincing.

---

1 See, for example, the author's "Effects of Music Education: Implications from a Review of Research," in *Perspectives in Music Education*, Source Book III, Music Educators National Conference, 1966.

Yet it is impossible to ignore the fact that a great many people have experienced their most satisfying, most fulfilling, most significant musical experiences *as performers,* and that at least some children who perform have had similar experiences. The power of such experience is so great and its satisfactions so deep that those who have shared it are likely to be changed fundamentally in their relation to music. For such people music inevitably becomes a source of some of life's deepest rewards. This is no small matter, given the universal need for such satisfaction and its rarity in human life. The question is, how can the performance program be so organized as to insure, as fully as possible, that genuine musical experiences will be fostered for all the children engaged in it?

Several factors can be identified which are essential to performance as aesthetic education. The first of these, paradoxically, is a necessary element in developing aesthetic sensitivity through performance and at the same time the major factor in limiting the aesthetic effects of performance. This is the factor of technical mastery—the control of an instrument or the voice to produce expressive sounds.

Obviously one cannot produce music without some medium for doing so, and to use a medium musically requires some level of skill. The major effort of children involved in performance is expended on skill development and the major focus of teaching is typically on this matter of technique. It can be argued, with undeniable force, that the ability to manipulate a complex object like an instrument or the voice at higher and higher levels of control is, in and of itself, one of the most pleasurable and rewarding of human activities. People have always found delight and meaning in mastery over materials. Anyone who has achieved such mastery, in any field of endeavor whatsoever, knows its satisfactions. Certainly the opportunity to develop musical mastery should be available to all children who would like to take advantage of it.

Yet mastery of technique cannot by itself justify the enormous effort expended by so many children in learning to play or sing. Most children, by the nature of human talent and societal needs, will never progress beyond modest levels of technical prowess. After the initial excitement of getting involved and showing some progress—an excitement which often lasts through the high school years—the child often begins to realize that there are diminishing returns on his investment of time and energy (not to mention money). Novelty turns into routine, excitement turns into boredom, the pleasures of progress diminish as limitations are realized. When the time comes that reinforcement by the social aspects of playing or singing in groups is no longer available, as when the student graduates, there is no longer any reason to continue with performance. Excluding the small number of children who achieve unusual success in technical mastery the large majority terminates any such activity as soon as the school conditions which fostered it are no longer present. Such children will have received some benefits, to be sure, but those benefits seem to be only minimally aesthetic. It is precisely because the situation described here is so prevalent that education now asks whether some more widely applicable value, some more unique value, some more lasting value, can be realized by the performance program.

Musical mastery, whatever its limitations when considered as a separate entity, must remain of concern to the performance program because little can be achieved if technique does not constantly improve. A second factor must be added, however, which transforms technique from sterility to fruitfulness as a means of aesthetic education. This is the factor of musical understanding—the perception of and reaction to the expressiveness of music. This is the central goal of music education, to which performance must contribute if it is to be regarded as a central part of the enterprise. And the fact is that performance can contribute to musical understanding in such important ways that its value can not be questioned.

When a child is producing music by playing or singing, either alone or in a group, and when his technique is being used in the service of producing sounds expressively, his understanding of the musical content of the piece he is performing can be very strong and very immediate. His actual involvement in producing the sounds, his responsibility for doing so musically, his intimate physical and mental contact with the expressive events, his necessarily intense focusing of musical perception and reaction as the music proceeds, all add up to a high level of musical understanding. The amount and quality of music's expressiveness revealed through musically-oriented performance can be as high as or higher than any other mode of musical experiencing. The systematic cultivation of musical understanding through the mode of performing is the major task of the performance program. To the degree that performance increases the musical understanding of the children involved, the program is successful as aesthetic education.

How can the performance program fulfill its aesthetic function consistently and efficiently? Most performance directors are genuinely concerned to give their students as musical an education as is possible. But just what does one do? How does one teach performance to make it aesthetic in its effects? It is one thing to make a group sound good. In this, performance directors have great expertise. If they feel the need to increase their skills as technicians in producing fine-sounding performances a vast number of workshops, college courses, institutes, clinics, are available for the purpose. No one questions the value of such activity.

Indeed, a performance director who is deficient in the skills of musical production can not begin to be an effective aesthetic educator. Of course an individual's or a group's performance must be technically adequate and of course the teacher is responsible for helping it be so. The question is, how does one fulfill that obvious and necessary obligation and at the same time fulfill the obligation to musical understanding; that is, to aesthetic sensitivity?

The first thing that can be said—very safely said—is that performance will not develop musical understanding automatically. Musical understanding must be consciously, systematically, carefully *taught for*. The disappointing lack of aesthetic insight resulting from typical school performance experience can not be attributed to performance as such but to the use of performance for non-aesthetic and pre-aesthetic purposes. Aesthetic sensitivity as even a peripheral goal, let alone the main goal, has rarely been aimed for in a conscious way. Instead, the assumption has been that teaching non-aesthetically would somehow produce aesthetic results. As in every other aspect of teaching in the arts this simply does not occur. It can be *made* to occur, however, by following the same principles which make education aesthetic in all facets of teaching and learning the arts.

The first of these—that music of high quality be the main material of study—is as relevant to performance as to any other aspect of music education. Much music performed in the schools in the past and to some extent in the present can only be described as abominable. Insipid in structure and vapid in expressiveness the musical diet of thousands upon thousands of children has led to an inevitable aesthetic malnourishment. But rather than dwell on the obvious and painful musical anemia of the school performance literature as it has been and remains today in far too many instances, it is much more pleasant to acknowledge the great gains which have been made in the use of genuinely valuable musical material. Some school systems have insisted on using excellent music for many years, and these stand as models for what school performance literature can and should be. The general level of the literature has risen remarkably in recent years, so that it is no longer unusual for performance programs to exhibit sophisticated musical tastes and it is no longer possible to argue that good music is just not available. The fact that one can honestly accentuate the positive in this matter should be heartening for all music educators.

Music of high quality need not be music of high complexity. Of course much music is inherently too difficult for most school groups but enough material of merit exists that every grade level in every school system can find musical rewards in the repertoire appropriate for its technical capabilities. For each separate performing group the literature studied should contain the same range of complexity as described for the general music program in the preceding chapter. There should be some pieces which present few if any technical or musical problems, some which are very challenging technically and musically, and most which can be performed and understood adequately but which contain enough challenge to warrant periodic study over a long period of time.

But while the overall shape of the repertoire is similar to that of the general music program some differences do exist. Because of the technical limitations imposed by performance the spread from easy to difficult will be smaller for any particular performing group than for a general music class, which is much freer to wander among musical extremes. Within this somewhat narrower curve of complexity individual children can be placed according to their capabilities as these are evolving, so that the more advanced performers have more musical responsibility, etc. One of the difficult tasks of the performance director is to see to it that the children in a particular group are receiving a reasonable balance of musical satisfaction and musical challenge, through a combination of the music used by the entire group and the individual's responsibility within the group. This is a most delicate but most important responsibility. It is often not capable of being met entirely within the context of a single performing group, in which some homogeneity of ability is needed so that talented performers are not unduly held back by very limited performers, who in turn are not constantly frustrated by demands they can not meet. At each grade level (upper elementary, junior high, senior high) an ideal performance program in regard to appropriateness of musical challenge would provide 1) a reasonable spread of ability groups in each performance medium, 2) a reasonable curve of musical complexity for each group, 3) optimal responsibility for each child within each group. Certainly this takes a skillful, sensitive, devoted teacher. Children deserve no less.

The technical and expressive complexity of the music used by performance groups has often not been determined by their members' musical needs but by the pressures of public performance. Concerts, contests, festivals, have a way of determining what music should be performed and how that music should be learned. Precisely the opposite should happen. That is, concerts and other public performances should be a natural outgrowth of the efforts of the group and its members, so that they can share with others the musical fruits of their labors. Suppose, for example, that a group is studying music containing a healthy diversity of challenge. Some of it can be performed with relative ease and full control, some cannot approach a public performance level, and much can be performed with enough control that musical satisfaction is being shared while at the same time re-study later would also prove satisfying. At reasonable intervals, depending on the best musical and educational interests of the group as determined by its director, public performances would demonstrate the abilities of the group with concentration on the music at the publicly performable part of the curve. Such performances, including contests and/or festivals, can be scheduled in advance because experienced directors know pretty much what will transpire during an average year.

Unfortunately, many performance directors labor under such severe pressure to perform often and well that their choice of music can only be determined by the single criterion of what their group can get ready in the time available. Business, after all, is business, and when the business of a performing group is considered to be performance the needs of music education become secondary. Many performance directors know full well that they are music educators only when time permits. Many want to cultivate musical understanding through performance as a major role rather than a minor one. Most know that an endless round of preparation for public performances does not produce aesthetic sensitivity except as an occasional byproduct. Many if not most performance directors, having the musical good of their children at heart, are ready to work toward a performance program which is primarily music education while at the same time satisfying in the matter of making music. Reflecting the aspirations of the music education profession and of education as a whole, performance can become—and in some instances already is—a model for what excellent education can be.

In addition to the factors of the quality and complexity of the music used, aesthetic education in music through performance will be based on the pedagogical principles discussed throughout this book. The sequence of learning—experiencing, studying, re-experiencing—is particularly pertinent to performance because of the very strong tendency to separate the study part of learning from the experience parts. This is especially the case in private study, where technique is often so isolated from musical experience that students can be unaware that there is a relation between the two. This also happens in performing groups when all effort is expended on whipping the music into shape and little time is left over for reaping the aesthetic benefits of the increasing technical control. When a student in his private lessons is laboring through exercise after exercise and in a performing group is constantly woodshedding, he is being starved of the aesthetic enjoyment which is the point of the entire enterprise. No wonder interest, joy, satisfaction, eventually disappear for so many children. Musical experience is so much more powerful in its grasp of the mind and feelings of people than sheer technique, that to neglect the one for the other is to miss the golden opportunity music presents for capturing the life-long devotion of those who are helped to glimpse its riches.

This should not in any way be taken as non-recognition of the necessity for serious work on technique. The question is not whether technical mastery should be developed but how its development can increase the availability of musical experience. Technical study can do so when it is closely allied to expressive music and is used in the service of expressive music. The closeness of technique to actual musical experience will vary according to the age and ability of the child, following the general rule stated previously (p. 116) that the size of the "experience-study-experience" pattern will grow as the child grows. At the beginning stages of performance one can not leave music, however simple the music, to dwell for extended periods of time on technique. The day of "stick with your exercises for a few years and then I'll give you a piece of music" has passed. It is an interesting and fortunate phenomenon that beginners in performance find musical pleasure in pieces far simpler than they would normally listen to for pleasure. So it is quite possible and necessary to provide musical satisfaction from the very beginning, with technique growing out of the problems presented by the music. The older and more proficient the student the less immediately related to an actual piece need the study material be. But no matter what the performance level, musical experience—the "pay-off" of musical study—must be amply provided if performance is to be musically educative.

In the study part of learning the performance director comes into his own as a music educator. The laboratory-like atmosphere of a performing group, in which the living stuff of music is right there to be handled, to be examined, to be manipulated, to be shared, is so educationally rich that it can be considered the best example of what meaningful education can be. There is no separation, in a performing group, of material being learned from the subject itself. The intimate contact with expressive sound provided by performance is the most valuable feature of this activity, offering unlimited potential for the development of genuine musical understanding.

To fulfill this potential the teacher must help his students, *primarily through the actual making of sounds,* to perceive and react to the expressiveness of the tonal events being brought to life. All the subtle shadings of perception which are fostered by musical analysis (exploration)—showing, manipulating, comparing, combining, contrasting, observing, clarifying, etc. (p. 121)—are immediately available to the teacher and his students in a performing group. Here is where the conductor becomes a "conductor-educator," as he skillfully reveals the living qualities of music to those who are giving recreative birth to it. By a sensitive balancing of technique and understanding, where each reinforces the other, the teacher can mold the perfect product—an expressive performance of deeply perceived and felt music. The more fully the performers grasp the musical content of a piece they are producing—its melody, harmony, rhythm, texture, etc.—the more fully can they share its musical meaning and the more musical can they make it sound. It is not often that one can have one's cake and eat it too. Good teaching in performance is one way this can be made to happen.

Materials are desperately needed which can help performance directors teach about the music being performed. As with listening materials, clever, musically honest and practical devices need to be developed which point out expressive musical events as they occur. Research and development projects dealing with this need should be of high priority for the music education profession.

The language used in performance settings as a tool for bringing musical conceptions and musical perceptions into contact with one another should be the same as that used in non-performing modes of studying music. The necessity of a common conceptual framework can be understood clearly when one thinks of the child who is in both a performing group and a general music class, as would ideally be the case for all children beginning with upper elementary grades. Each mode of learning reinforces the other. The general music class provides an *extensive* experience of music, conceptions and perceptions being developed over a very broad range of musical material. The performing group provides an *intensive* experience of music, the same conceptions and perceptions being strengthened through intimate contact with musical processes. Given a common language of musical conceptions and its development in both breadth and depth through the emphases of general music and performance, musical perception and the opportunity for musical reaction will have been optimally provided for every child.

If it is assumed that performance teachers should be aesthetic educators it must also be assumed that their education will have prepared them to be experts in developing aesthetic sensitivity through performance. Unfortunately, teacher education in music continues to be massively technique-oriented. College courses for undergraduates which attempt to give an understanding of the nature of the arts through a study of philosophical and psychological foundations of art are so rare as to be almost nonexistent. Methods courses, conducting courses, materials courses, all focus on techniques of effective production to the virtual exclusion of techniques for heightening musical perception and reaction through the mode of production. Music theory and history courses are usually totally separated from any concern with how what is being learned can be used in helping children to learn. Private applied study is aimed toward developing the performance abilities of each student with little or no attention to how similar development can aid the aesthetic insights of young people. Given few opportunities in his training to either consider what aesthetic education in music might be or to gain the tools for carrying on a music program which is aesthetic in nature, the performance director finds himself ill-equipped to become what he often wants to become—a good director *and* a good music educator.

The most potentially fruitful place to help the teacher-in-training become what he needs to be is the college performing organization. Here we should find a laboratory for learning how to teach for aesthetic sensitivity through the powerful mode of performance. Instead, one often finds performance for the sake of performance, the aspirations of the group's conductor being to develop as professional a sound as is possible with little regard for whether his students are learning through example how to use a group for educative purposes.

There should be no opposition between the technical-musical needs of college students and their needs as potential aesthetic educators. These needs are interdependent. It is time—high time—for the music education profession to concern itself with an equitable balancing of emphases in the teacher-education program.

When a performance program succeeds in being an aesthetic education program; that is, when good music of appropriate complexity is used, when musical experience is the major focus of effort, when the clarification of musical content is a natural and necessary part of the learning process, when musical mastery and musical understanding are both being pursued and are so balanced that each strengthens the other, performance can finally be considered to have fulfilled the conditions of excellent education. Musical talent will be fostered and enriched with musical intelligence, while musical understanding will be developed as a function of intimate involvement in tangible musical processes. When helped to achieve an integration of musical mastery with musical understanding at least some children will achieve a third value which transcends the benefits of both: they will have gained a sense of becoming *part of the act of aesthetic creation.* That experience is among the most fulfilling a human being can have, as all who have had it know full well. The fact that it is potentially available to every child as a natural outgrowth of participating in a musical performance program adds another powerful dimension of value to those already present.

To pursue the values of performance as aesthetic education systematically and vigorously has become a major task of the music education profession. The benefits of doing so can be very great—to the profession as a whole, to those responsible for the performance program, to every child who is or will be involved in performance activities. The aesthetic rewards are there in abundance. The job now is to reap them.

QUESTIONS FOR DISCUSSION

1. Can you think of other reasons than those given for the popular appeal of the performance program? What historical and educational movements and events have influenced the development of performance in the schools?

2. Do you agree that the performance program should be considered a basic part of music education as aesthetic education? What are some arguments for treating performance as strictly special education? What difficulties and opportunities are suggested by both views?

3. How has music education been affected by the heavy reliance on non-musical justifications for performance? What effects has "selling" rather than "justifying" performance had?

4. How solid and convincing is the available scientific evidence about the relation between performance and the development of aesthetic sensitivity to music? If one were to base one's conclusions on general experience rather than experimental evidence, what conclusions are likely to be reached about the degree to which performance 1) is now affecting, 2) can be made to affect, musical sensitivity?

5. Do you think it is possible to pay necessary attention to the development of performance technique and at the same time use technique in the service of musical understanding? Would doing so require a readjustment in typical performance teaching methods?

6. What are 1) the gains and 2) the losses from the public performance aspect of the performance program? How might one work toward progressively decreasing the losses and increasing the gains?

7. Do you agree that teacher education programs need adjustment if performance teachers are also to be aesthetic educators? What suggestions can you make for changes in the education of performance specialists?

8. Are you aware of any trends in the profession which indicate movement toward more concern about the aesthetic effects of performance? Any trends in the opposite direction? On balance, can you predict the general direction the profession might take in the near future?

CHAPTER TEN

music education as aesthetic education: music among the arts

The philosophical foundation for music education offered in this book is obviously applicable to all the arts even though its main emphasis has been musical. The discussion about the nature and value of music as an art can give helpful insights for teaching every art, either separately, as covered in the previous two chapters, or together. In recent years a great deal of interest has been shown in courses—usually at the high school level but often at lower levels as well—which attempt to teach several arts together. Such courses offer unique opportunities for developing aesthetic sensitivity. They also raise severe problems about practically every aspect of education and aesthetics. On the one hand, pedagogical problems multiply astronomically when more than one thing at a time is taught. On the other hand, philosophical problems become immeasurably more complex when the relations among similar subjects are brought into the picture. The combination of these two factors produces an immensely thorny educational thicket.

Curriculum researchers have for many years gone to extraordinary lengths to keep out of the thorns of multi-subject approaches. The large majority of educational reform efforts in our time have been expended on single subjects, with much concern that the integrity of each subject be recognized and protected. This was especially the case in the earlier years of the curriculum reform movement, when problems of rethinking educational goals and strategies were so pressing that the addition of combined-subject problems would have been intolerable. As experience was gained in developing acceptable approaches in single subjects, efforts to combine subjects began to appear. Such efforts are never taken lightly. Curriculum researchers have very often been the most sophisticated, most knowledgeable, most thoughtful educators our society has ever produced. They know full well the magnitude of multi-subject problems, unlike those who assume that it is a simple matter to teach several things at once. It is little wonder that such a great gap exists between the very few carefully researched multi-subject approaches, which give indications of exciting educational potential, and so many of the multi-subject courses in actual use in the schools, which are such a disappointment to those able to seriously evaluate them. The closing of this particular gap is an important task for education in the near future.

In the arts both the dangers and the benefits of combined approaches are high. Philosophically the arts present problems of interrelations which are at least as difficult—if not much more so—as any other subject area. Educationally the problems in the field of art are very complex for each art singly but much more so when arts are combined. At the same time the potential gains in aesthetic insightfulness from dealing with more than one art at a time are great enough to warrant efforts in the direction of combined courses. How can these gains be made while avoiding the dangers of superficiality, of confusion, of aesthetic simplemindedness, of weakening rather than strengthening the impact of art? The comments offered in this chapter are intended as a sketch of some possible guidelines for use in working toward acceptable answers to this question.

A few basic principles about the arts and their interrelations need to be stated at the outset. One of these is that the differences among the arts are much more fundamental than are their apparent similarities. The division of the realm of art into several arts is by no means a product of modern-day compartmentalization or specialization. The distinctiveness of the various modes of art has been recognized throughout history by every serious thinker in aesthetics. Many attempts have been made, with varying degrees of success, to explain how the arts relate to one another. The fact that these relations have always been and continue to be difficult to explain should make it clear that we are dealing with much more than a simple or artificial problem. In fact, it is precisely because the differences among arts are genuine and deep that the domain of art is so richly diverse, so capable of continual growth and change, so productive of new and different satisfactions. The diversity of art is a major aspect of the delight of art. To revel in that diversity, to pursue the many roads to aesthetic enjoyment, to increase one's sensitivity to the various modes of artistic expressiveness, is to take full advantage of all that the many arts have to offer.

Are the arts, then, so different that they can not be compared? The deeper one goes into the essential nature of each art the closer one comes to the shared nature of all art. Beyond the differences among the arts is that which makes all of them "art." All art serves the same function, which is to provide a means for exploring and understanding the nature of human feeling. All art fulfills this function in a common manner, which is to embody, in some perceptible medium, conditions which are analogous to the conditions of feeling. All art yields insights into feeling through the same mode of sharing, which is to perceive the conditions expressive of feeling and to react to their affective power.

Aesthetic education is the systematic attempt to help people explore and understand human feeling by becoming more sensitive to (better able to perceive and react to) conditions which present forms of feeling. Such conditions are potentially present in everything but are created solely for that purpose in works of art, which is why the study of art is the major—but not the exclusive—way to improve aesthetic sensitivity. In each art, education which attempts to increase aesthetic sensitivity to that art can be called "aesthetic education." In any combination of arts, education which attempts to increase aesthetic sensitivity to each one of the arts included can be called "aesthetic education." Whether treated separately or together the goal of teaching art aesthetically remains the same; to make more shareable the insights into subjective reality presented by each and every art.

To realize this goal, the distinctive ways that each art operates must become progressively clearer. One can not become more aesthetically sensitive except by becoming more aesthetically sensitive to sounds, to colors, to shapes, to movements, to verbal images, to spaces, to actions. Each of these has its unique ways to do what all of them do. Art has unlimited potential for exploring human feeling *because* of the uniquenesses of each art mode, not *in spite of* them. Glossing over the uniquenesses, diluting them by forced combinations, dulling them by constant equating of one with another, making them more obscure by ignoring the peculiar, particular flavor of each, can only weaken aesthetic sensitivity and limit the capacity to share aesthetic insights in the wide variety of ways they are available.

What, then, can courses in more than one art accomplish which courses in each single art can not? The value of multi-subject approaches is their ability to 1) make each subject clearer by showing its uniquenesses as contrasted with other subjects in the same family, 2) clarify the underlying principles which make all the subjects members of the same family, 3) give a broad view of each subject as an individual in a family and of the family as one among many. These are important values, well served by combining subjects in a single course of study. But any such course must avoid the dangers of 1) submerging the character of each individual by focusing exclusively on family likenesses, 2) assuming that surface similarities show up underlying unities when in fact they usually do not, 3) neglecting specific perception-reaction experiences in favor of a generalized, disembodied "appreciation of the arts," 4) using non-artistic principles to organize the course in order to give an impression of unity. An approach which emphasizes the unique flavor of each art but at the same time demonstrates why each art is "art" should yield the advantages of a combined arts course while avoiding its dangers. This general principle is an outgrowth of a point of view summarized nicely in the following excerpt from a lecture by Susanne K. Langer:

> If we start by postulating the essential sameness of the arts we shall learn no more about that sameness. We shall only skip or evade every problem that seems, offhand, to pertain to one art but not to some other, because it cannot be really a problem of Art, and so we shall forcibly limit ourselves to simple generalities that may be safely asserted. . . . My approach to the problem of interrelations among the arts has been the precise opposite: taking each art as autonomous, and asking about each in turn what it creates, what are the principles of creation in this art, what its scope and possible materials. Such a treatment shows up the differences among the several great genera of art—plastic, musical, balletic, poetic. Pursuing these differences, rather than vehemently denying their importance, one finds that they go deeper than one would expect. Each genus, for instance, creates a different kind of experience altogether; each may be said to make its own peculiar primary creation. . . . But if you trace the differences among the arts as far and as minutely as possible, there comes a point beyond which no more distinctions can be made. . . . Where no more distinctions can be found among the several arts, there lies their unity. . . . *All art is the creation of perceptible forms expressive of human feeling.*[1]

Before making some suggestions as to how the principles briefly sketched above can be applied to education, some current practices in arts

---

[1] *Problems of Art*, pp. 78–80. Italics are Langer's. The chapter from which this excerpt is taken is entitled "Deceptive Analogies: Specious and Real Relationships Among the Arts." This short chapter summarizes much of Langer's thought on how the various arts are and are not related. It is "must" reading for anyone connected in any way with inter-arts courses.

courses need to be reviewed. Several additional principles should emerge from doing so.

One approach to inter-arts classes is to study works in which materials from several arts have been used. This approach often includes attempts by students to produce works which combine materials from several arts. The assumption is that music with words, dance with music, drama with visual elements and/or music, etc., all illustrate how several arts can be combined to make something larger than any single art. In such an approach "allied arts" is taken quite literally—the alliance of several arts is assumed to be the best illustration of and means of entry into the realm of "art."

In fact, however, works which use materials from art domains other than their own, as many works do, can be successful only to the extent that the added materials become completely fused in the characteristic materials of the host art. A musical setting of a poem, for example, is purely musical in a successful work because the music "swallows" the poem and transforms it into another element in the musical expressiveness. To the extent that the two—words and music—retain separate aesthetic identities the work is disunified, ambiguous, incomprehensible as either music *or* poetry. It will be remembered from several discussions in previous chapters that non-artistic elements (conventional symbols such as a program in music, representation in painting, political statements in drama, etc.) become aesthetic elements when they become submerged in the aesthetically expressive conditions of the work in which they are used. If a work does not succeed in assimilating the non-aesthetic contents into its expressive form the work is incomplete and weak, the non-artistic material obscuring the work's artistic import. The same principle applies to the use of artistic materials borrowed from other arts. When successful, music plus words equals music. Dance plus music equals dance—*purely* dance, *completely* dance, "unadulteratedly" dance—for the music has become assimilated by bodily movement and no longer is experienced separately as musical. It is quite possible, of course, to listen to the music separately, as on a recording of ballet music, and regard it purely as musical. When it is used in an actual dance production, however, it reverts to its status as an expressive element in the impact of dance as dance.

This "principle of assimilation" applies to any and all of the arts.[2] Whatever the material borrowed, whatever the amount of borrowing, the primary mode of expressiveness of each art continues to be the determi-

---

[2] For detailed explanations of this principle, with many examples from all the major arts, see Langer's *Problems of Art,* Chapter 6, and *Feeling and Form,* Chapter 10, "The Principle of Assimilation."

nant of the total experience. In recent years a great deal of borrowing has taken place from art to art, just as in both the past and the present much borrowing from non-artistic sources has taken place in every art. Heavy borrowing always makes aesthetic success more chancy, but the criterion for success remains what it always is—that *everything* in a work of art must contribute to the structural excellence and expressive power of the work's unified aesthetic presentation. We are learning now that old notions of "proper" materials for each art were often too narrow, in that each major art domain seems to be able to assimilate a great deal of material from other sources without necessarily being compromised or diluted. Also, several separate arts have been used in simultaneous presentations, as in "happenings" or "multi-media" events. The success of such presentations is a matter for honest debate, some people finding them effective, others not.[3] As with other problemmatical new practices in the arts aesthetic educators have an obligation to share new ideas freely and openly, using them as opportunities for rather than threats to the development of aesthetic sophistication. But whatever the means, the ends of aesthetic education are well served when sensitivity to *each mode of expressiveness* is the basis for teaching and learning.

Attempts to produce works using materials from more than one art are likely to be unsatisfying in education because of the extremely high levels of creative insight required to produce such works successfully. But more important is the serious hazard of indulging in invalid practices such as "combining" arts by translating a piece of music into a painting, a dance into a poem, a sculpture into a dance, etc. These can only yield disastrous results: artistically because genuine aesthetic creation is impossible when conceived as a transference of expressiveness from one medium to another; educationally because of the false impression given of how the arts work and what aesthetic experience is like. Certainly the impulse to create, often called "inspiration," can come from anywhere and anything. But once begun, aesthetic creation depends on involvement in the developing expressive form *in the particular medium being used.* If that involvement is strong and expert, material from other media can be used in and fused with the primary medium. But to think that one either experiences or learns about the nature of more than one art at a time because a particular work uses more than one kind of material, or that one can experience or learn about the nature of more than one art at a time by transposing one art into another, is to misunderstand art and to subvert the process of art education.

---

[3] Langer's skepticism is illustrated by her famous quip "There are no happy marriages in art—only successful rape" (*Problems of Art,* p. 86).

Several other current practices in the arts must be reviewed before more satisfactory practices can be suggested. The most common means of organization in multi-arts courses are 1) the "historical" approach, 2) the "topical" approach, and 3) the "common elements" approach. All sorts of combinations of these exist, of course, but a discussion of each will apply to their combinations as well.

The historical approach views the arts as a product of the conditions existing in the world at various times. It is usually organized chronologically but need not be so, some people preferring to work from the present backwards or to jump from one period to another which is distant in time or to juxtapose two or more periods. Whatever the organization the emphasis of study is similar—the work of art as an object in a particular context. The assumption underlying this approach is that everything—art included—exists in context, and that to understand a thing one must understand its context. To understand a work of art one must know about the social, political, religious, psychological, physical, etc. conditions existing in the world at the time the work was produced.

It is not surprising, given this assumption, that historically oriented arts courses include a great deal of non-artistic subject matter—often to the virtual exclusion of actual works of art. There is ample precedent in education for assuming that knowledge about backgrounds inevitably illustrates foregrounds. The traditional "liberal arts" or "humanities" curriculum was (and is) primarily a historical-philosophical study in which interest in works of art was primarily in their historical-philosophical aspects. Performance, composition, painting, dancing, acting, analysis, were not proper for the liberal arts course, but could be safely relegated to "applied" studies. A "humanistic" education consists of knowing about influences: of studying ideas, theories, principles. The tangible, objective, explorable, unique qualities of particular objects are quite secondary to the generalized context in which the objects exist. The *background is* what the humanistically educated man knows. And the more one studies the background the more "humane," supposedly, does one become as an individual.

This old argument has become less and less convincing over the years as the existence of "universals" has become very questionable and as the contributions to human life of applied fields has become undeniable. The "humanities" have insisted that they are the road to wisdom, to goodness, to truth. But they have been strikingly unsuccessful in demonstrating precisely *how* they lead to these goals.[4] Too often wisdom is

4 An interesting discussion of this point is W. David Maxwell, "A Methodological Hypothesis for the Plight of the Humanities," *AAUP Bulletin*, LIV, No. 1

equated with information, goodness with a genteel life-style cultivated in certain academic circles, truth with skillfulness of argument.

The position taken in this book has been that what is humanising about art is the *experience of* art rather than *knowledge about* art. When art is experienced aesthetically it gives, to the extent it is good art, as powerful, as effective, as tangible a sense of the human condition as is available to human beings. *This* is humanistic. *This* is what transforms experience from mundanity to meaningfulness. *This* is what adds the dimensions of significance, of insightfulness, of self-knowledge, of "wisdom" if you will, to human experience. The arts are humanistic to the extent they are *directly* known: to the extent they are aesthetically experienced. Aesthetic education is humanistic if and when it increases the sensitivity of people to the aesthetic qualities of things.

Certainly background information can contribute to the aesthetic perception of and reaction to works of art. This is precisely the role of such information—a *contributory* one. When helpful, when germane, when necessary, historical, social, philosophical, political, etc. information should be used, but only to the extent that it actually does contribute to the aesthetic experience itself. While this extent can not be stipulated as a generality, it can be safely asserted that historical approaches usually are much overburdened with non-artistic information and are puny in actual experiences of particular art works. History as history is a necessary, important field of study. So are philosophy, religion, languages, etc. But so is aesthetic education. In aesthetic education first things should come first.

One of the common arguments for the historical approach is that works of art are "expressions of their times," and that if one understands art one also understands a great deal about the period in which that art was produced. Several difficulties exist in this argument. First, the use of art works as indicators of a period's fashions, social customs, manners, etc., while perfectly valid if one is studying social history, is quite beside the point if one is concerned with aesthetic education. The information about a period's social mores contained in representational works is often taken to be the reason for studying such works. Many "educational" films about art, for example, consist almost entirely of information about the "life of the times," using paintings as *illustrations*. The artistic value of the paintings is seldom if ever mentioned, except to admire the technical skill required to produce this or that effect. Small wonder that so many

(March, 1968), 78–84. Two responses to a slightly revised version of Maxwell's article are given in *The Journal of Aesthetic Education*, III, No. 2 (April, 1969), 81–89.

people think they understand art when they can recognize its cultural references, and are so puzzled by works which contain no such references. The treatment of art as illustration is a mainstay of the "art appreciation racket." Aesthetic education had better be something more.

Another argument for art as an expression of its time is somewhat more sophisticated but still unconvincing. This is the notion that a work of art reflects the underlying social forces of its period. As the social milieu changes because of wars, inventions, scientific discoveries, new philosophies, etc., art changes accordingly. The study of art is largely a tracing of influences, all the arts of a period giving a record of the major historical events of the period.

Aside from the non-aesthetic orientation of this approach it also suffers from a gross oversimplification of the facts. To the extent that a work is artistically self-sufficient it is not often necessary or possible to connect it with non-artistic matters. And it is even more difficult to try to lump together all the arts of a period as if they all were directly influenced by the same forces and all reflected those same forces. As Leonard Meyer explains:

> . . . it is a mistake to insist upon coordinating style periods among the several arts, or upon relating style periods to political or social history. Events may coincide or they may not. . . . Historical facts do not support a theory of "direct" causation. Extra-stylistic "forces" do not in themselves appear to be either necessary or sufficient causes for style change . . . the course of stylistic change is not invariably and directly affected by changes—even major ones—in other facets in the cultural environment . . . though the "arts" have a family resemblance, there are important differences between them which affect not only our perception and understanding of them but also the ways in which they tend to develop. This being true, there is no compelling reason for assuming that the several arts necessarily develop at the same rate or in the same way (or, that their developments reflect that of the culture generally).[5]

Still another assumption connected with the historical approach is that art reflects the emotional tone of an era. If one can sense the characteristic emotional flavor of the art of a period one can understand how people of that period felt about themselves and their world. There is an element of truth in this idea but several dangers as well. The most obvious is that of falsifying the facts by selecting just those works which tend

---

5 *Music, the Arts and Ideas* (Chicago: University of Chicago Press, 1967), pp. 92, 93, 109, 114. By permission of The University of Chicago Press. © 1967 by the University of Chicago.

to support the theory. For example, many people argue that modern music "expresses" the unique way that modern life feels. The tensions, the anxieties, the uncertainties of modern life find their natural expression in music. To such an assertion one might reply, "Do you have in mind, for example, Aaron Copland's *Billy the Kid* or *Appalachian Spring?*" "Oh, no," would be the answer. "I didn't mean that." "Well, how about Howard Hanson's *Romantic Symphony?*" "Certainly not. *That's* not what I meant either." "Then perhaps you mean something like Menotti's *The Unicorn, the Gorgon and the Manticore?*" "Well, of course not." "How about Schoenberg's *String Quartet No. 4?*" "Ah! That's *exactly* what I meant. *That's* modern music!"

It is very easy to oversimplify by thinking that previous periods were devoid of the same immensely varied expressive flavors as our own. One seizes on particular works, identifies their mood quality, and then extrapolates to all other works and to the period as a whole. This glosses over the richness and diversity of art at *any* time in history, and gives the impression that each art is expressive in the same way as the other arts, and that within each art all the works have the same general expressiveness. It is really the *differences* one should explore, however—the differences from art to art and from art work to art work. To do this, it is little help to say that a period's characteristic emotion-tone will emerge as the sum total of all the productions in art of that period. This statement says so much it says nothing. One *can* help students become sensitive to the style characteristics of each art in each style period, by showing how the expressive elements of each art were used in peculiar ways at various times in history. As they become more sensitive to the changing style modes of the various arts their sensitivity will help in pursuing the central goal of any convincing approach to aesthetic education—to be able to share more deeply the particular, unique, incomparable expressive power of individual art works in many arts and many styles.

All the weaknesses of the historical approach add up to the possibility that aesthetic education, when conceived as "the history of art," will be singularly ineffective in developing aesthetic sensitivity. Art works are most worthy of study when they transcend their own time of creation. A good work presents possibilities for insights which are relevant to humans at any time. The deeper the expressiveness of a work the more it remains a living, vital source of aesthetic meaning, capable of sharing that meaning with all people. One might argue that the job of aesthetic education is to *rescue* art works from their historical contexts: not to deny that every work does indeed have a context, but to concentrate on those qualities which make the work ahistorical. Background material can help if used wisely. Stylistic exploration is an absolute necessity. But it is doubtful that an approach suffering from any or all of the difficulties mentioned here can fulfill the aesthetic needs which aesthetic education exists to serve. Art should not be primarily conceived as a way to understand other times, but as a way to understand our own lives.

The second popular approach in inter-arts courses, the "topical" organization, uses as the means for allying the various arts such topics as "Man and Nature," "The Quest for Freedom," "The Idea of Democracy," etc. The Referentialist basis of this approach is obvious. The arts are conceived primarily as statements—as attractively gotten up arguments, as emotionalized commentary, as vehicles for non-aesthetic ideas, attitudes, beliefs. The meaning of art can be found in the subject matter of art. If one chooses works in different arts according to some similarity of subject matter one can show how the subject has been treated in various ways yet at the same time maintains its essential character. A landscape painting, a poem about flowers, an "outdoor" novel, a "pastoral" piece of music (you can tell it's pastoral by the oboe and flute duet), all illustrate "Nature," showing how different artists "expressed their feelings and ideas" about a common subject. The arts can help people learn about Nature, about Democracy, about a multitude of topics. Art, then, is a most useful means toward non-artistic ends.

There are so many problems with this approach that to deal with them in detail would necessitate an application of all the material in Chapters Two through Seven. At this point it should be quite clear that under any non-Referential view of art the assumptions underlying the topical approach are unacceptable. This approach reduces art from expressive form to conventional symbol; gives the impression that non-representational works are meaningless; tosses out all but the most programmatic music (which is why the music teacher in this approach usually winds up giving his own, separate little course); chooses art according to non-aesthetic criteria; equates work with work and art with art as if a similar subject negated the uniqueness of art works; focuses the attention of students away from art's aesthetic content toward its non-aesthetic content; subjugates aesthetic meaning and experience to non-aesthetic meaning and experience. The point need not be belabored. To the degree there is merit in the position about art taken in this book the topical approach is to that degree without merit.

The "common elements" approach organizes the study of the arts around units on "rhythm in art," "form in art," "unity and variety," "the use of contrast," etc. This kind of organization does call attention to intra-artistic matters rather than extra-artistic matters, so at least has the merit of being aesthetic in orientation. Unfortunately, however, it often has the effect of leveling aesthetic sensitivity rather than heightening it.

This occurs because of the danger of neglecting differences in favor of similarities. It is often assumed that because the same word is used to name phenomena in several arts that therefore the phenomena must be the same. If music contains rhythm, if poetry contains rhythm, if painting contains rhythm, if dance, sculpture, even architecture contain rhythm, then one need only demonstrate how rhythm is essentially the same in all these arts in order to demonstrate that all of them are manifestations of the same process. When one adds form, contrast, variety, etc., the arts begin to merge and blend together into a homogenized, undifferentiated whole.

The more one concentrates on what seem to be similarities the further one gets from fundamental differences which lie below the surface. Rhythm in music, for example, is both a product and a cause of a multitude of sound characteristics which are peculiar to the mode of aural stimuli. The musical "apparition" or "semblance" of sound events perceived as expressive is a world with a flavor of its own, "laws" of its own, affectiveness of its own. Rhythm in painting is a product and cause of a host of visual characteristics which are very powerful because of their uniquenesses. Similarly for poetry, dance, etc. The question for aesthetic education is not "What is rhythm as the sum total of all its uses?," but instead, "What makes rhythm in music *musical,* what makes rhythm in poetry *poetic,* what makes rhythm in dance *what it peculiarly is in dance?*" Obvious similarities among artistic elements need not be ignored, of course, just as obvious similarities of subject matter or mood need not be ignored. The crucial issue is how these similarities are used. If they obscure diversities they can only impoverish the experience of art. If they are used as opportunities for probing uniquenesses they can heighten aesthetic sensitivity by developing more subtle, more discriminating, more responsive perceptions of the richly divergent modes of aesthetic expressiveness.

Solutions to the problems of inter-arts approaches must overcome the weaknesses of many present courses yet not abandon the concept of dealing with all the arts together. So much is to be gained in the way of expanded aesthetic sensitivity through what might be called "General Aesthetic Education" (to distinguish multi-art courses from aesthetic education in each single art) that serious curriculum efforts in this direction should be wholeheartedly supported by each art field. Such efforts, involving qualified researchers, teachers, scholars and practitioners from all the arts, will hopefully eventuate in several good options from which schools can choose as they seek to expand their offerings in aesthetic education. While such work has been and is now going on, the magnitude of the problem calls for continuing and expanded effort.

It would be presumptuous to imply that a small portion of a single book could solve a problem of the size being discussed. Yet, having criticized several accepted practices, and having implied that better things are possible, an obligation exists to point out at least some directions for improvement. The following suggestions are intended to 1) be consistent with the philosophy developed in this book, 2) avoid the weaknesses enumerated above, 3) identify the major common dimensions of the arts, 4) preserve the individuality and integrity of each art, and 5) provide a framework within which various kinds of inter-arts courses, involving various combinations of arts, at various levels of schooling, can be generated. What is offered, then, in necessarily brief and sketchy fashion, is a kind of "mega-model" for general aesthetic education.[6]

The major dimensions common to all art are 1) the people involved in the aesthetic realm, 2) the behaviors they employ, 3) the shaping of artistic elements by expressive means, 4) the qualities and processes used in aesthetic functioning, 5) various constraints on aesthetic possibilities, 6) the art-work, in a particular style, which is a product of 1)-5). Each of these dimensions will be explained in turn.

The people of primary concern to aesthetic education are the CREA-TOR, the RE-CREATOR, and the EXPERIENCER. The creator is a composer, a painter, a poet, a choreographer, a playwright, a sculptor, an architect, etc. All of these people are engaged in the same activity—searching out and discovering expressive qualities of things and embodying them in perceptual form. All of them create precisely the same thing: embodiments of the forms of subjective reality. But their creations exist within different expressive realms, giving distinctive meanings to the subjective according to their own views. Each creator shines a different light on human feeling, illuminating it with the color of his own mode of insight. There is, therefore, a large common element and a large element of uniqueness in aesthetic creation.

The re-creator is a performer, conductor, dancer, actor, director, etc. All of these people are engaged in the same activity—transforming the unactualized aesthetic insights of the creator into actuality. All of them begin with a set of instructions and all take the responsibility for carrying out the instructions wisely and well. All share a common goal—the bringing of artistic expressiveness to life. Each, however, has his own, peculiar

---

[6] This model is an outgrowth of the author's involvement as Music Education Specialist for the Aesthetic Education Curriculum Program, a research program sponsored by the Central Midwestern Regional Educational Laboratory, Wade M. Robinson, Executive Director. The author is most grateful for the help he received from the other members of the staff in articulating the model and refining its content.

mode of doing so. Some arts use no re-creator and in some arts the distinctions between the creator and re-creator can be blurry or non-existent (jazz, improvisational theater, etc.). Re-creation in art, then, involves many common elements and many distinctive elements as well.

The experiencer is the person who listens to music, watches a play or a dance, reads a novel, looks at a painting, etc. In every case the experiencer is searching out the expressive conditions in the thing to which he is attending and sharing the sense of feeling those conditions embody. The searching out process involves the same general behaviors no matter what the art (see below), but the *content* of the experience changes from art to art reflecting the distinctive expressive conditions of each art. For any single art work experiencers will share common insights into feeling presented by the work's expressive conditions, and at the same time gain insights peculiar to each experiencer as an individual. Many common elements and many distinctive elements are present in experiencing art, as is the case in creating or re-creating art.

The three aesthetic roles described are of course interdependent, a single person being quite capable of being all three at once or one at a time. Our interest, however, is in the characteristics which make each role identifiable.

Seven major behavior categories are relevant to the arts and aesthetic education. Two of them—PERCEIVING and REACTING—may be considered central. The others—PRODUCING, CONCEPTUALIZING, ANALYZING, EVALUATING and VALUING—support and enrich aesthetic perception and aesthetic reaction. Each behavior category contains many sub-behaviors, some of which are common to several main categories. A sample of sub-behaviors is as follows. *Perceiving:* recognizing, recalling, relating, observing, identifying, locating, comparing, etc. (see p. 81). *Reacting:* feeling, emphasizing, attending, responding, sensing, undergoing, absorbing, etc. *Producing:* adding, balancing, forming, including, manipulating, preparing, generating, combining, controlling, etc. *Conceptualizing:* naming, recounting, reporting, speculating, writing, stating, defining, discussing, conjecturing, etc. *Analyzing:* showing, imitating, comparing, rearranging, modifying, classifying, characterizing, locating, examining, etc. (see p. 121). *Evaluating:* appraising, accepting, rejecting, rating, preferring, judging, ordering, pairing, deciding, etc. *Valuing:* approving, choosing, accepting, favoring, liking, excluding, etc.

In addition to these general behaviors—general to all the arts and to teaching all the arts—there are some special behaviors relevant to each art. These include singing, conducting, playing, acting, reciting, moving, writing, rhyming, carving, printing, drawing, designing, etc. As one goes deeper into the technicalities of each art the behaviors become more particular and narrow: bowing, fingering, breathing, etching, mixing, splicing, flexing, parsing, mimicking, etc. The most general behavior with each art, of course, is the aesthetic experience of it, consisting of perceiving and reacting as in listening to music, watching a play, reading a poem, etc. While elements of conceptualizing, analyzing, evaluating and valuing might be present in aesthetic experience (especially the overlapping qualities of valuing and reacting), they need not be present and in fact can interfere with free, open aesthetic sharing. When used in the *service* of aesthetic perception, however, they are indispensable tools.

While human behaviors are always more complex and subtle than the words available to name them, the above list can serve as a reminder of the many ways (however interdependent) that people—creators, re-creators, experiencers—relate to art. The primary concern of general aesthetic education is with the major behavior categories common to all the arts, although the distinctive behaviors peculiar to each art will be used as necessary to support the common ones. Within the common behaviors the *content* will change from art to art. The content of perception is quite different in music and sculpture, even though the same behaviors are brought to bear on each. The content of analysis is quite different in poetry and dance, even though the same behaviors are used to analyze each. Similarly for each behavior category, each sub-behavior, and each art.

Every art work is a product of artistic ELEMENTS which have been used according to expressive MEANS. Each art has its own primary elements: melody, harmony, rhythm, etc. in music; color, line, texture, etc. in painting; metaphor, verbal imagery, rhyme, etc. in poetry; and so forth (compare p. 52). Each art can borrow elements from the others, assimilating them into its own domain. And many arts can use elements from the non-artistic world, transforming them into expressive material by using them artistically. All elements in art are manipulated according to means which bring the elements to expressive life. These means include tension, relaxation, uncertainty, deviation, repetition, contrast, development, direction, imitation, dimension, regularity, dynamics, shape, speed, density, connotation, allusion, balance, weight, etc. Many means are common to several arts (tension, repetition, direction, etc.) but their *content* is different according to the art using them. Direction in music, in dance, in architecture, for example, has distinctive characteristics according to the primary expressive impact of each of those arts. Some means tend to be more limited to single arts than others (modulation as in music, muscle tension as in dance, scenes as in drama, open space relations as in architecture). Combinations of means used in recognizable ways yield overarching, organizational means: sonata allegro, rondo, sonnet, masque, tragedy, portrait, collage, mobile, etc. The commonality of the arts in this dimension consists of their common dependence on elements and means. The uniqueness of the arts, and of each single art work, is a result of particular elements used by particular means. Again, common aspects and unique aspects are present.

In order for art works to be created and shared several QUALITIES and PROCESSES must be present. Qualities of imagination, of sensitivity, of craftsmanship, of spontaneity, of originality, of dexterity, etc. are required by every artist in every art. Many of these qualities are required in order to experience any art. The *content* of each quality changes from art to art, however, according to the particular requirements of each art. Craftsmanship in music has its own demands, as does craftsmanship in theater and in dance and in sculpture. The common quality, then, is manifested distinctively in each art.

Aesthetic processes are the broad modes of operation stemming from the qualities of artists and governing the use of elements and means. These processes include exploring, building, pattern-using, unifying, embodying, planning, etc. Again, each art depends on these general processes, but the *content* of each process varies from art to art. "Building" in a novel is one thing; in dance it is quite another. As with all the other dimensions, the focus in teaching about aesthetic qualities and processes should be on their common existence but their unique manifestations.

Every work of art reflects various constraints exerted on creators, recreators and experiencers. Artists and experiencers of art are to some extent free to do what they will and to some extent constrained by forces beyond their control. Some constraints stem from the nature of the artistic materials of each art. Sound, for example, can do certain things but not others. Above and below certain pitch levels human auditory capabilities begin to taper. Color has vast potential for artistic usefulness but not unlimited potential. Canvas, brushes, oils, impose tangible restrictions on what a painter can do. The human body is a marvelously expressive instrument but it does have built-in limitations. Every art must work within the limits—however widened by technology and knowledge—of that which is possible.

Similar constraints are inherent in artistic elements and means, many stemming from the particular style in operation at the time an artist lives and works. Musical form in the Baroque could not be what musical form became in the late nineteenth century. Painting in the sixteenth century could not use devices available to the Impressionists. The poetic imagery of the twentieth century is quite different from that of the eighteenth. Every aspect of every art is similarly constrained by matters of "possibility." All such constraints, because they are closely connected to the actual materials of art and how those materials can be used, may be called INTRA-AESTHETIC CONSTRAINTS.

A great many less directly artistic constraints exist as well. When Mozart was commissioned to compose a Requiem he could not very well set out to create a Divertimento for woodwinds. Political constraints have determined much of the output of contemporary Russian art (and of art at many times and in many places). Social constraints, economic constraints, psychological constraints, technological constraints, etc., have played their part in what art has been and can be. Such forces, which may be called EXTRA-AESTHETIC CONSTRAINTS, can be studied in such a way that they add to aesthetic insight. They can also be studied as phenomena divorced from particular experiences of particular works, so that they become of academic interest rather than aesthetic interest. When used as a means of clarifying the expressive nature of works being explored, an understanding of the constraints imposed on the works can indeed help aesthetic sensitivity grow.

The outcome of all the dimensions explained above is the actual ART WORK, which is always in a particular STYLE. As mentioned in the discussion of the "historical" approach, generalizations about style, when they cross over from one art to another, must be made with extreme caution. Just because the arts coexist in time does not necessarily mean they can be equated in style at any particular time. Also, one must not overemphasize similarities of style from one art to another, for aside from the most superficial of similarities (such as a certain haziness in Impressionistic painting and music) there is really not a great deal which can honestly be said to be comparable. When similarities exist they may of course be pointed out, but the fruitful area of study is each art's characteristic uses of its expressive elements at various times in its history. It is possible to treat the arts of an era together if one does not force them to be more similar than they are. The teacher should remember that the goal of instruction is keener sensitivity to *each* art, rather than a disembodied "appreciation of art." Art exists only in the tangible instances called art works: the word "art" is *only* a word. Appreciation or sensitivity can not be of a word—it must be of the tangible things to which the word refers. Nothing is gained by a compulsion to force each art to give up its individual existence in favor of the idea of "art." When the aesthetic educator turns his attention and the attention of his students to actual aesthetic objects and events he can begin to heighten the enjoyment of them without feeling that the enjoyment will increase if he somehow makes them merge. A sense for style is a necessary condition for grasping the insights of works in different styles, but this can be developed without constant equating of style with style. As in every other dimension shared by the arts, the existence of style is common to all but manifested distinctively by each.

The common dimensions of the arts may be put into the form of a model, as an aid in constructing units of instruction. The following is one form such a model might take:

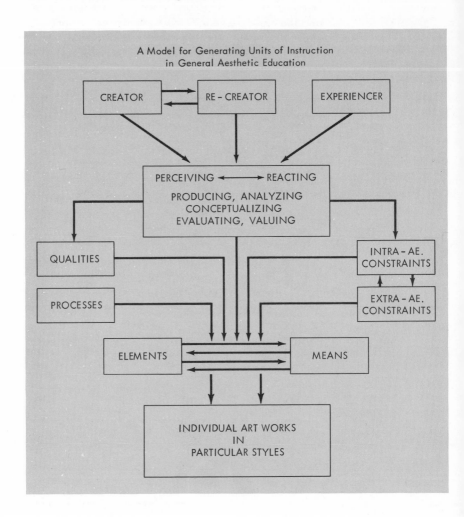

A Model for Generating Units of Instruction
in General Aesthetic Education

In this model the people involved in art are shown as relating to all the dimensions of art through the major behaviors used in the realm of art. (The two-way arrows between creator and re-creator indicate the indistinctness of these functions in certain instances.) Qualities, processes, intra and extra-aesthetic constraints (the two-way arrows between constraints indicate that it is often impossible to distinguish between them), all impinge on the creation, re-creation and/or experience of art. The actual use of artistic elements by expressive means is the heart of the creative process and the focus of aesthetic experience (the two-way arrows indicate the interdependence of elements and means). Out of all the interacting forces is born the actual work of art in its particular style.

Units of instruction can begin with *any box* in the model and with *the relations among boxes*. In every case, the boxed words are the *common dimensions among the arts*. The *content* of each dimension, however, and the *relations* among dimensions, must be allowed to be what they actually are for each art, with no attempt to force similarities in content or relations.

Suppose, for example, that a unit of instruction is desired which illustrates the quality of craftsmanship as a necessary one for creating art. Suppose further that this unit is for grades 3, 4 or 5, depending on the abilities and background of the actual children to be taught, and that it will involve music and drama. A sequence of activities, using various behaviors (only the most obvious ones will be named), might look like this:

The children are asked to clap (produce) a succession of quarter notes. They are then asked to clap (produce) again, adding accents to some of the notes. The children notice (perceive) the interest (react) created by the added accents. They discuss (conceptualize) their finding and hypothesize (conceptualize) about why the accents add musical interest. They explore (produce, perceive, react) different accent patterns and decide (conceptualize, evaluate) which they think are most interesting (evaluate, value). They are then asked to consider (conceptualize, evaluate) how they might notate (analyze, conceptualize) the best examples so they can be performed again at some later time. The children discover (perceive) the difficulties involved in translating musical ideas into notational equivalents, and discuss (conceptualize) skills of notation as one kind of craftsmanship a composer must have. They then listen (perceive, react) to a complex, rhythmic excerpt from a piece by Stravinsky. A score of the music is examined (analyze, perceive) as an instance of just how much skill is involved in notating complex music. The children discuss (conceptualize) the craftsmanship Stravinsky exhibits (evaluate, value) and hypothesize (conceptualize) about how all composers must have similar craftsmanship.

Now some of the children are asked to improvise (produce) a scene on a given situation. They observe (perceive, analyze) the lack of coherence (evaluate, react) because of a lack of stage directions. They discuss (conceptualize) the need for some means of giving directions if the scene is to make sense. They then explore (analyze, conceptualize, perceive) different ideas for giving the actors directions. The children discover (perceive, conceptualize) the need for a language which is understandable and exact, and which gives clear indications of what the participants are to do. They read (perceive, react) the stage directions given by a skilled playwright and discuss (conceptualize) whether the language seems to be what is needed (evaluate, analyze). They hypothesize (conceptualize) about how all playwrights must have skills of giving clear directions by using language in craftsmanly ways. They discuss (conceptualize) the quality of craftsmanship as being necessary to create music and drama successfully, and note (perceive, analyze) that there are interesting differences in craftsmanship in music and in drama. Finally, they hypothesize (conceptualize) that each art probably calls for its own kind of craftsmanship.

Obviously, many other sequences of activities could be generated, involving many other arts, using various behaviors more intensively than others or balancing them in various ways, each sequence leading to a more sensitive grasp of craftsmanship in the realm of artistic creation. The sequence could be contracted to take just a few minutes or expanded to occupy a few weeks. It could be simplified for younger children or made more sophisticated for older children. It could incorporate other aspects of craftsmanship in addition to "notation" or it could be followed by similar sequences dealing with other aspects of craftsmanship to form a larger unit. The limitations are the ingenuity of the teacher or teachers, the capacities of the children, the time available and decisions as to how to use it wisely, and the nature of the arts themselves, which must always be honestly and accurately dealt with.

Units of instruction similar to the one suggested could easily be developed to illustrate craftsmanship as a factor in *re-creating* art. Instead of "notation" the focus could be on various ways a song or a dramatic speech can be performed, with a rich blend of perceiving, reacting, producing, analyzing, conceptualizing, evaluating, valuing, brought to bear on the problems of craftsmanship involved in artistic re-creation. The outcome, again, would be a more sensitive understanding of craftsmanship as a factor in all re-creation, and the different ways it is manifested in each performing art.

Still another sequence could be developed dealing with craftsmanship as a factor in *experiencing* music and drama (and the other arts). Here various strategies would illuminate the difficulties of hearing everything going on in a piece of music or in observing everything going on in a play, etc. The outcome would be a deeper grasp of craftsmanship as a necessary attribute for enjoying *all* art, and of the various kinds of crafts-manship required in order to enjoy *each* art.

One further example, briefly presented, will have to suffice at this point. Suppose a unit of instruction was desired to illustrate effects of non-aesthetic contraints on aesthetic production, and that the students in question are 11th and 12th graders. For the sake of brevity let it also be supposed that the arts involved are, again, music and drama. The teach-ing-learning process might take the following form (the major behavior categories will remain only implied):

The students listen to an orchestral piece containing Russian patri-otic and folk tunes. They discuss the theory of Socialist Realism as it affects the composer's choice of melodies, the amount of harmonic com-plexity permissible, and the effect of using melodic association on the pos-sible forms the piece can be cast in. They compare the work to others like it and discover the existence of common patterns used by several composers of such music. They discuss the effects of Socialist Realism on freedom of musical choices, and hypothesize about the bases for artistic choice when no such theoretical constraint is present.

The students then read or, if possible, watch, a scene from a Russian play which illustrates various folk-ways and social attitudes. They apply understandings from the discussion of music to the play, discovering non-artistic constraints to be present again and hypothesizing about how such constraints determine the form, action, imagery in the play and how these elements might be determined if constraints were absent. The class then divides into a "composer group" and a "playwright group," the first sketching the outlines of a Socialist Realism opera, the second building an outline of a Socialist Realism play. The groups then share with the entire class their product and the problems they encountered while making it, performing bits and pieces of their work if time and talent allow.

Now the class turns its attention to a piece of music composed under WPA auspices during the Depression years, and to a play written under the same circumstances. They discover that here, too, extra-aesthetic con-straints are in operation, shaping and molding the art works in ways not purely aesthetically determined. After noting how such constraints im-pinge on how artistic elements can be used, and the qualities needed in order to satisfy extra-aesthetic demands in an aesthetic context, the stu-dents again try their hand at "creating" according to some of the con-straints they have discovered in operation. They share the results, and discuss how artists in various places and at various times might have had to work under conditions which did not encourage total aesthetic freedom. Their discussion might end with a tentative hypothesis, to be explored in further units, that the more non-aesthetic the constraints imposed on an artist the less likely it is that he can create works which are aesthetically self-sufficient and exploratory.

This entire unit can be used as a basis for exploring non-aesthetic constraints on re-creators and on experiencers. It can be compressed into a single class period or expanded into a semester's course of study. It can include any and all the arts as well as aesthetic qualities of non-art products and activities. It can use many production activities or none at all. It can cover a wide variety of works in different styles or concentrate on a few works in a single style. The possibilities for fruitful aesthetic learnings are very great, even within the context of this single choice of common artistic dimensions and their relations.

When one adds all the possible choices and combinations suggested by the model, as applicable to any and all grade levels, any and all arts, any and all aesthetic qualities of the non-art environment, using any and all behaviors and various strategies by which the behaviors can be clustered, one begins to get a sense of how much can be done to heighten aesthetic sensitivity through tangible, active, involved, teachable, learnable activities in general aesthetic education. The arts *can* be taught in ways which benefit from their being studied collectively, while at the same time their individuality is not compromised. The task at present is one of curriculum development—of putting into sensible form the possibilities for learning so richly present in the field of the arts.

Curriculum development is a complex job, but it can benefit from the wealth of experience generated in recent years. Several principles from the area of curriculum reform are particularly pertinent to general aesthetic education. The first is that an understanding must exist of the fundamental nature of the subject in question, and that courses of study must focus major effort on the subject's fundamental nature. This book, it is hoped, provides one viable position about the nature of art, which can be used as one basis for organizing curricula. While practically everything covered in this book has bearing for teaching the arts, Chapter Eight, The General Music Program, is particularly pertinent. The principles suggested there for general music are almost entirely applicable to general aesthetic education. The reader might review that chapter, reading it with all the arts in mind rather than music alone. It would be found that the guidelines for aesthetic education mentioned at the ends of Chapters Three through Seven, and applied in Chapters Eight and Nine, are extremely useful for the organization of teaching and learning in the several arts. That works of high quality be used—that is, works of structural excellence and expressive impact: that the experience of art come first and last: that major attention be paid to the objective qualities of art which are aesthetically expressive: that conceptualization be true to art as a whole and to each single art: all these fundamental principles can serve as tangible guidelines for action. The diagram on p. 123 is perfectly suited to general aesthetic education: the only change would be that each arrow would stand for each art (with another arrow for the aesthetic qualities of non-art), with the seven major behaviors implied for each art. The major idea—that all arrows point toward the common goal of deeper aesthetic perception and reaction (deeper aesthetic experience)—is the same whether one art or all the arts are being taught.

Another applicable principle from curriculum reform is that courses should follow a tight, logical sequence of topics, in which each thing studied is generated by the previous topic and leads inexorably to the next, all of them revolving around the major conceptions of the course. One such sequence of topics in an inter-arts course might begin with the people involved in the arts and their behaviors, qualities and processes. This would be followed by a unit on the elements and means of each art. The final unit would deal with artistic style, including intra and extra-aesthetic constraints which bear on style possibilities. Many other sequences are suggested by the model for general aesthetic education.

Curriculum reform has demonstrated the necessity for the development of high quality instructional materials which can be used in a variety of educational settings. The need for effective materials in general aesthetic education is basic and pressing. Some materials are being generated by various projects, but the newness of the field and the complexity of the problem have made production only partially successful. It is obvious that major projects are needed to develop excellent materials embodying defensible alternative approaches to teaching the arts.

Finally, curriculum reform has made clearer than ever before that good education ultimately depends on good teaching. The entire problem of teacher education for general aesthetic education must be given serious attention in the years ahead if this field is ever to become more than a pleasant dream. Are courses in the arts to be limited to high schools and taught by existing specialists in the single arts? Or would they be taught by newly developed personnel equipped to do the job by themselves or with the help of single-art specialists? Are elementary and junior high schools to be included in general aesthetic education? If so— and ideally that will be the case—will classroom teachers have to assume major responsibility or will specialists have to be trained or will some combination of the two prove to be the most feasible? Are teacher education institutions willing and/or able to inaugurate curricula for general aesthetic education? Will team teaching be necessary or can individuals hope to be effective in this field? What effect will emerging patterns of general aesthetic education have on teachers in service and programs in operation in the separate arts?

Surely the one thing this field does not lack is interesting and complex problems, only the most obvious of which have been mentioned. But the magnitude of the problems is matched by the magnitude of the possible values to be gained. The values of art and of aesthetic sensitivity are their unique service to that which is most human about human beings— the capacity for self-understanding and the need for significance. If art can thus serve *any* human beings, it can serve *all* human beings. The charge and the mission of aesthetic education—whether in a single art or all the arts—is to improve the aesthetic quality of every person's life at every stage of his development. Aesthetic education can fulfill its promise only by being an operative, flesh and blood field of active teaching and learning. The measure of support and dedication given to the task of making it so—in every art and in all art—will be an accurate measure of the maturity of our social system. For there is no better gauge of a society's concern for the quality of its members' lives than its level of concern for the arts and the teaching of the arts. Aesthetic education lies at the core of a humane society.

QUESTIONS FOR DISCUSSION

1. What are some of the built-in hazards of multi-art approaches? What are the potential benefits? Would you characterize multi-art courses with which you are familiar as being 1) very hazardous, 2) very beneficial, 3) a mixture of both?

2. In as specific terms as possible, discuss 1) real differences among the arts, 2) the level at which the arts may be said to be "the same." Do you agree that the quite common view of the arts as being "the same" at all levels is a superficial one?

3. Why is a distorted view of art likely to be given by concentrating on works which use elements from several arts? What is the danger of having children "combine" arts by translating one art into another?

4. As you think of multi-art approaches with which you are familiar, or as you examine course descriptions from various sources, can you categorize most courses as either 1) historical, 2) topical, 3) common elements, 4) some combination of those three? Discuss the weaknesses of the courses according to the weaknesses of each approach. Do any aspects of the courses seem to overcome the inherent weaknesses?

5. Try to formulate different curriculum-generating models than the one given, using the same cells (common dimensions) within each model. What are some advantages and disadvantages of each model? Can you think of other cells which might be added?

6. Try to generate various units of instruction from the model given, including several combinations of arts and several levels of schooling. How can separate units be combined into a unified course of study? Can you conceive a plan for a "mega program," including all the arts from grades 1 through 12?

7. Do you think that a total General Aesthetic Education Program, encompassing all the arts taught together at all grade levels, is within the realm of possibility at any time in the foreseeable future? What are the obstacles to such a program? Do you think the potential benefits call for a major effort to bring such a program about?

index

formalist — intellectualism

plndy = sounds

referentalist — communistic meaning outside art
emotional art = "of life" good person = good art

signals   m3 =

absolutist — qualities in work itself

expressionist — middle ground
meaning + value of art in works
but relation of art to life must be seen